A SOCIAL HISTORY OF THE RUSSIANS AND THEIR ARMY SINCE 1690

Russian Shorts

Russian Shorts is a series of thought-provoking books published in a slim format. The Shorts books examine key concepts, personalities, and moments in Russian historical and cultural studies, encompassing its vast diversity from the origins of the Kievan state to Putin's Russia. Each book is intended for a broad range of readers, covers a side of Russian history and culture that has not been well-understood, and is meant to stimulate conversation.

Series Editors
Stephen M. Norris, Professor of History, Miami University, USA
Polly Jones, Professor of Russian, University of Oxford, UK

Editorial Board
Edyta Bojanowska, Professor of Slavic Languages and Literatures, Yale University, USA
Ekaterina Boltunova, Associate Professor of History, Higher School of Economics, Russia
Eliot Borenstein, Professor of Russian and Slavic, New York University, USA
Melissa Caldwell, Professor of Anthropology, University of California Santa Cruz, USA
Choi Chatterjee, Professor of History, California State University, Los Angeles, USA
Robert Crews, Professor of History, Stanford University, USA
Dan Healey, Professor of Modern Russian History, University of Oxford, UK
Polly Jones, Professor of Russian, University of Oxford, UK
Paul R. Josephson, Professor of History, Colby College, USA
Marlene Laruelle, Research Professor of International Affairs, George Washington University, USA
Marina Mogilner, Associate Professor, University of Illinois at Chicago, USA

Willard Sunderland, Henry R. Winkler Professor of Modern History,
University of Cincinnati, USA

Published Titles

Pussy Riot: Speaking Punk to Power, Eliot Borenstein

Memory Politics and the Russian Civil War: Reds Versus Whites,
Marlene Laruelle and Margarita Karnysheva

Russian Utopia: A Century of Revolutionary Possibilities,
Mark D. Steinberg

Racism in Modern Russia: From the Romanovs to Putin,
Eugene M. Avrutin

Meanwhile, In Russia: Russian Internet Memes and Viral Video,
Eliot Borenstein

*Ayn Rand and the Russian Intelligentsia: The Origins of an Icon of the
American Right*, Derek Offord

The Multiethnic Soviet Union and Its Demise, Brigid O'Keeffe

Nuclear Russia: The Atom in Russian Politics and Culture,
Paul Josephson

The Afterlife of the "Soviet Man": Rethinking Homo Sovieticus,
Gulnaz Sharafutdinova

*The History of Birobidzhan: Building a Soviet Jewish Homeland in
Siberia*, Gennady Estraikh

The Soviet Gulag: History and Memory, Jeffrey S. Hardy

Why We (Still) Need Russian Literature, Angela Brintlinger

Russian Food since 1800: Empire at Table, Catriona Kelly

Jews under Tsars and Communists, Robert Weinberg

Gulag Fiction: Labour Camp Literature from Stalin to Putin,
Polly Jones

Russian Culture under Putin, Eliot Borenstein

How Russia Got Big: A Territorial History, Paul W. Werth

Soviet Internment: Memory, Nostalgia and the POW Experience,
Maria Cristina Galmarin

*Racism in Modern Russia – Revised Edition: From the Romanovs to
Putin*, Eugene M. Avrutin

Russia's Arctic: Climate Change, Domestic Policy and Geopolitics,
Marlene Laruelle and Jean Radvanyi

A Social History of the Russians and Their Army since 1690,
Roger R. Reese

Upcoming Titles

Russia's History Painters: Vasily Surikov, Viktor Vasnetsov, and the Remaking of the Past, Stephen M. Norris
Black Encounters with the Soviet Union, Maxim Matusevich
The Invention of Russian Time, Andreas Scholne
The Tolstoy Marriage, Ani Kokobobo

A SOCIAL HISTORY OF THE RUSSIANS AND THEIR ARMY SINCE 1690

Roger R. Reese

BLOOMSBURY ACADEMIC
LONDON • NEW YORK • OXFORD • NEW DELHI • SYDNEY

BLOOMSBURY ACADEMIC

Bloomsbury Publishing Plc, 50 Bedford Square, London, WC1B 3DP, UK
Bloomsbury Publishing Inc, 1359 Broadway, New York, NY 10018, USA
Bloomsbury Publishing Ireland, 29 Earlsfort Terrace, Dublin 2,
D02 AY28, Ireland

BLOOMSBURY, BLOOMSBURY ACADEMIC and the Diana logo are
trademarks of Bloomsbury Publishing Plc

First published in Great Britain 2026

Copyright © Roger R. Reese, 2026

Roger R. Reese has asserted his right under the Copyright, Designs and
Patents Act, 1988, to be identified as Author of this work.

For legal purposes the Acknowledgments on p. xii constitute an
extension of this copyright page.

Series design by Tjaša Krivec
Cover image: Saint Petersburg, Russia - April 27th, 2009: Three Russian
soldiers listening to a guitare player while having a break, left one eating at
the moment; the photo taken by The Church of the Savior on Blood between
The Neva and Nevsky Prospekt © Ababsolutum / iStock

All rights reserved. No part of this publication may be: i) reproduced or
transmitted in any form, electronic or mechanical, including photocopying,
recording or by means of any information storage or retrieval system without
prior permission in writing from the publishers; or ii) used or reproduced in
any way for the training, development or operation of artificial intelligence
(AI) technologies, including generative AI technologies. The rights holders
expressly reserve this publication from the text and data mining exception as
per Article 4(3) of the Digital Single Market Directive (EU) 2019/790.

Bloomsbury Publishing Plc does not have any control over, or responsibility
for, any third-party websites referred to or in this book. All internet addresses
given in this book were correct at the time of going to press. The author and
publisher regret any inconvenience caused if addresses have changed or sites
have ceased to exist, but can accept no responsibility for any such changes.

A catalogue record for this book is available from the British Library.

A catalog record for this book is available from the Library of Congress.

ISBN: HB: 978-1-3502-3648-6
PB: 978-1-3502-3647-9
ePDF: 978-1-3502-3649-3
eBook: 978-1-3502-3650-9

Series: Russian Shorts

Typeset by Newgen KnowledgeWorks Pvt. Ltd., Chennai, India
Printed and bound in Great Britain

For product safety related questions contact productsafety@bloomsbury.com.

To find out more about our authors and books visit www.bloomsbury.com
and sign up for our newsletters.

For Helen and Soren

CONTENTS

List of Figures	x
Preface	xi
Acknowledgments	xii
A Note on Transliteration and Names	xiii
List of Abbreviations	xiv
Introduction	1
1 The Lives of Soldiers	5
2 To Serve or Not to Serve	33
3 The Officer Corps	57
4 Society, the Military, and the State	81
Conclusion	107
Notes	109
Select Bibliography	125
Index	129

FIGURES

1.1	Days of revolution—troops on the Liteinyi Prospect. Saint Petersburg, Soviet Union Russia, 1917	13
1.2	Soldier of the Army of the Russian Federation taking the oath of service	17
1.3	Red Army soldiers in the USSR (Union of Soviet Socialist Republics), Russian Federation, 1941?	22
1.4	An action organized by the Latvian Women's League at the Freedom Monument in Riga, 1989	29
2.1	New conscripts entraining to report for duty	38
2.2	Volunteers for the front, 1917	44
3.1	Bain News Service, publisher. Russian Army officers, *c.* 1910 (between and *c.* 1915)	62
4.1	Russian youth participating in military summer camp	92
4.2	*Iunarmiia* youth marching in the annual Victory Day parade	93

PREFACE

It is hard to write a short book. More is left unsaid than said. With that in mind, this book seeks to evaluate more than 300 years of history to help the reader comprehend the Putin regime and its war with Ukraine and to understand Russian society's relation to its army. But by necessity, it must be limited to one major theme: the continuity of Russian military culture and the ramifications. The roots of Russian military culture run so deep and entwined with the political culture that they have enabled the military to remain fundamentally unchanged in their outlook, through the monumental social and political upheavals of the rise and fall of the communist experiment. This book outlines the basic features of that military culture, how it was formed and became entrenched despite the attempts to change it. One of the underlying explanations for the lack of lasting change, more tacit than explicit, is the idea that Russia's regimes, whether the tsarist semi-feudal autocracy, the Soviet totalitarian communist, or Putin's pseudo-democratic authoritarianism have exhibited a remarkable ability to withstand popular demands for change. Emancipating the serfs and subsequent military reforms operated within, rather than challenged, military culture. The revolution that brought down the tsar that led to the Soviet experiment in creating a classless society did not, in the long run, truly change the military culture or the military leadership's relationship with society. The failure of that experiment had no effect on military culture whatsoever.

Because such a long period of history is being addressed, much of the work is a synthesis of the best scholarship. I rely on secondary sources written by some of the field's most prominent scholars, especially for the seventeenth and eighteenth centuries. The primary sources for the twentieth and twenty-first centuries consist in large part of the periodical press, which I hope I have used judiciously. Because much of the material used for the twenty-first century is available online, readers can look them up and decide for themselves what to make of them.

ACKNOWLEDGMENTS

First and foremost, I thank my wife, Melora, for her support and forbearance during the years-long process that writing a book entails. I, once again, express my gratitude to Tamara Chapman for her expert editing and insightful comments that helped focus my thoughts. I thank Jonathan Brunstedt for alerting me to the opportunity that Bloomsbury presented with this series on Russia. I owe the history department of Texas A&M University my thanks for granting a semester off to complete my research. I also thank the Texas A&M University Association of Former Students for sponsoring a Faculty Development Leave, giving me a semester off from teaching to finish the manuscript.

A NOTE ON TRANSLITERATION AND NAMES

This work follows the Library of Congress transliteration system, without diacritical marks to transliterate Russian personal names, place names, and other words. For reasons of familiarity and historical context, I used Russian spellings for names and places as they existed in the time period. During the course of my research, I used translated works with a wide variety of transliteration styles, all of which I converted to the Library of Congress system when making direct quotes in order to establish some consistency and not confuse the reader. In these cases, the transliteration system of the original author is kept intact when identifying the published work in the notes and bibliography. Exceptions to this general style are words and names that are likely well known to the reader rendered in other transliteration systems.

ABBREVIATIONS

ARCMW	All-Russian Council of Mothers and Wives
CSM	Committee of Soldiers' Mothers
DOSAAF	All-Union Voluntary Society for Assistance to the Army, Air Force, and Navy
GlavPUR	Main Military Political Administration
NVP	Preparatory Military Training
OSOAVIAKHIM	Society of Friends of Defense, Aviation-Chemical Construction
UCSMR	Union of Committees of Soldiers Mothers of Russia

INTRODUCTION

Armies are not only organizations tasked with advancing a nation's interests by force of arms, but they are also institutions that can play either positive or negative roles in society, and yet the Russian peoples have had a persistently conflicted relationship with their army from its earliest days that most often accentuates the negative aspects characterizing military service as a burden, misfortune, or even catastrophe. Still, most accept the need for an army, and as an institution it has been respected in the abstract. This book examines the varying relationships among, and expectations of soldiers, officers, and society related to military service to answer questions that are especially relevant today, as an authoritarian Russian Federation deploys its military in costly and unpopular wars. Just why have the men of Russia been so averse to serving, and why have their families been so reluctant to let them go to the military? Why has the military been so slow to act in its own best interest and address its recruitment and retention challenges? Why has it failed—persistently and dramatically—to foster a culture that instills pride in service, creates career opportunities for soldiers, and cultivates support from the Russian public at large? And finally, what has this failure cost the state, as it pursues its goals and ambitions?

This book examines military service and its impact on both soldiers and families in three successive political orders: tsarist Imperial Russia and its brief constitutional years, the communist Soviet Union, and the current Russian Federation. The salient themes are the economic and emotional effects of service on soldiers' families; conditions of service and how they affected soldiers' and society's view of service; the dynamic of attempts by society to hold the military accountable for its treatment, care, and use of soldiers; and the officer corps' culture of resistance to accountability. This work advances three arguments: first, that though the political system changed three times and the various regimes did want the people to support military service, no Russian government has taken their people's aversion to the military seriously enough to make the changes that would alter public opinion; second, that since the 1861 emancipation of the serfs, the Russian people have expected the army to treat its soldiers better and have increasingly sought to force the army to change its behavior, thus exacerbating an already adversarial relationship; third, for much of its history, the successive Russian states have been largely successful in militarizing the economy and government, attempts to militarize *society* have been consistently contested by the masses. Although some of the most intense efforts to militarize society belong to Vladimir Putin's regime, it has served to increase resistance, particularly since the onset of his war with Ukraine. Finally, this book shows that the Putin regime has enabled the historically worst practices of the military in its treatment of soldiers and relations with civil society to thrive in the current era.

This work explores the expectations and behaviors of the army's leaders from the top down—from generals to ensigns—and how they related to each other, their soldiers, and civilians. From the bottom looking up, this book delves into the expectations, behaviors, and feelings about service of the enlisted men and how these changed over time. Outside the military, civilian attitudes toward the military are examined to reveal their expectations of the army, their willingness or unwillingness to serve, and their views of the army as an institution. Views run the gamut, from those who see the army as an oppressive body enforcing the will of the elites and the state, to others who view it as a symbol of patriotism. Throughout, the agency of all members of society and the army and the degree to which they used it to serve their interests, are emphasized.

Tsar Peter I codified the regulated police state in Russia, in which the private interests of individuals were sacrificed to the common good. In the manner of France's Louis XIV, Peter and the many tsars and tsaritsas who came after him thought of themselves as the state. They marshalled the human and material resources of the state to pursue the collective good as they defined it. The Muscovite roots of the autocracy enabled Peter I to institutionalize *boyar* (noble) subservience to the tsar—servility so extreme that nobles called themselves the sovereign's slaves—in a system that produced a militarized service state. In this militarized state,

Introduction

the nobles owed a life of service to the throne, and the rest of the people were the property of the state. The fundamental idea was that the people served the autocrat, not vice versa. Peter I entrenched this thinking during the imperial period and it subsequently found expression in the Soviet era, when the people served the Communist Party-run state. The idea that the people owed the state service was briefly and weakly challenged between 1991 and 1999, only to be rejuvenated by Vladimir Putin, who styles himself a twenty-first-century tsar.

The idea that the people owed the state their service and unquestioned loyalty, as well as the notion that they had no right to hold the state accountable, meshed neatly with the mindset of the military leadership. The officers—who owed life service to the tsar and state until the 1760s and had no right to question or refuse the tsars' commands—naturally extended this principle to the lower ranks. Once in the service, soldiers owed their officers unquestioning obedience. Families had no right to question the tsars' or army's use of their men. This thinking was adopted by the Communist Party during the Soviet period. In the twenty-first century, the state still promotes the idea that the people are obligated to serve it and that it has the right to conscript men—although the Russian people now do question the army's use of their men, which greatly annoys the officer corps. The officer corps generally has successfully thwarted attempts to hold it accountable, but at the expense of its credibility and loss of trust. The sense that the state has the right to compel service, that the bodies of its people are its property, and that the army is above reproach arguably have been and continue to be the bases for conflict between society and the military for more than a hundred years. It is also arguable that if the military leadership simply treated its personnel humanely, this conflict would decline significantly.

Written from a social- and cultural-historical perspective, this book does not qualify as traditional military history, in that it does not address battles and campaigns or strategy and tactics. Instead, a major aim of this book is to offer insight into how military service was experienced by its members; how army culture has been shaped by internal and external expectations; and how Russian society's relationship with the army transitioned through dramatic regime changes and shifting ideological imperatives as Russia modernized

Social History of the Russians and Their Army

socially, politically, and economically. The tension among the people, the state, and the army, and between the soldiers and the army, is a thread that runs through the chapters ahead, as does the issue of accountability, most often spearheaded by women. Since the 1980s, the contest between the people's attempts to hold the army accountable for its maltreatment of soldiers in peace and wanton disregard for their lives in war has persisted, as have the army's efforts to condition the people to accept military service as a duty without question through patriotic education, propaganda, and claims of military necessity.

By bridging the historical eras of serfdom, post-emancipation late-imperial Russia, Soviet Russia, and contemporary Russia, this book analyzes the broader aspects of the social history of the Russian military and firmly situates the army within society and the Russian narrative. This is the first English-language work to examine the broader aspects of the social history of Russians and their military from the late seventeenth to the early twenty-first century. It breaks new ground by firmly situating the army and its personnel within a complex society that confronted a range of issues associated with modernization. A study such as this is important because, unlike a study of the army at war, it gives a picture of the military's stature and influence, and of its relationship with the people who staff and support it. It helps us understand its socially based performance and challenges on the battlefield and the military's often uneasy relationship with society at large and even the state itself.

Chapter 1 details the lived experience of military service and illustrates the often-inhumane conditions that continue to provoke resistance and aversion to service in the modern era. Chapter 2 addresses the Russian peoples' aversion to service and how they have exercised agency to avoid it. Chapter 3 examines the military leadership's relations with the soldiers and society, as well as its expectations of both. It is telling that these expectations have remained remarkably consistent from the seventeenth century to the twenty-first. Chapter 4 explores the interrelationships of society, the military, and the state in the context of each entity's competing visions and expectations. Along the way, it analyzes the state's attempts to militarize society from the early twentieth century and the people's resistance to them.

CHAPTER 1
THE LIVES OF SOLDIERS

Across the centuries, the Russian soldiers' overall experience of service has been negative. This chapter argues that this negative experience is the most important factor that has and continues to alienate the Russian people from the army. Taken from their families and civilian lives against their will, soldiers typically see themselves as victimized, anonymous cogs in a huge machine in peacetime, and as cannon fodder in wartime. The soldiers' self-image as variously, proud servants of the tsar, state, nation, or people has had to compete with their experience as victims of the state whose primary goal was to survive their term of service and then get on with their lives. The material quality of life (quartering, nutrition, pay) for soldiers has usually been low. For peasants, it was often indistinguishable from their civilian situations. Soldiering has mostly been a brutal experience at the hands of their non-commissioned officers (NCOs) and officers. Training naturally is physically demanding, and the hours outside of training can be mind-numbingly boring. Life on campaign is exhausting and carries the risk of death or crippling injury.

Using individual and collective initiatives, soldiers have taken what measures they can to ameliorate their conditions, but most resign themselves to the powerlessness of their situation at the hands of uncaring superiors. In peacetime, soldiers unable to bear unfair or harsh treatment have exercised agency by deserting, committing suicide, or murdering those who cause their misery. In times of war, they have also shirked, sought capture, and gone over to the enemy. These behaviors have been most pronounced since the end of the nineteenth century. Comradeship and alcohol have helped soldiers cope with the stresses of army life, but racial, religious, ethnic, national, and language differences have caused rivalries within military units that sometimes turn violent, even deadly. Since the mid-1960s, the phenomenon of hazing (*dedovshchina*) has undermined solidarity and created antagonism among soldiers of different draft cohorts. Except for a brief period from 1923–39, service in the Russian army, for the enlisted ranks, mostly has been characterized by physical and psycho-emotional suffering.

The Identity/Self-Image of Soldiers

Up until the emancipation, when a serf was conscripted, his social category changed; he was no longer a serf, but a free man though one bound in service to the tsar. On discharge from the army, he retained his freedom. This was far more than a legal nicety. Soldiers did, after a time, internalize their new identity and saw themselves as a distinct social group separate from their civilian origins. With the end of serfdom and the length of service set at six years, the social category of soldier disappeared, and conscripts retained their pre-induction social status. A radical change in how they understood their identity resulted. Soldiers no longer saw themselves as the sovereign's property or a separate social class. Instead, they began to see themselves as citizens serving the nation, not just the autocrat, in a relationship of reciprocal obligation.

A challenge then arose for the military leadership: how to get soldiers to shed their civilian outlook and identify as soldiers for their time in the army. The officers generally expected the men to adopt the mentality and ethos of soldiers—to see themselves as servitors of the tsar, detached from civil society—as they had before the emancipation. For the most part, through indoctrination and forcing the men to obey institutional norms, this expectation was met up to the Revolution of 1905. With the advent of the Soviet state, and the short two-year term of service, the Red Army struggled to get the men to identify as soldiers. The rank and file largely kept their civilian outlooks. In the post-Soviet era, with conscripted service of only one year, conscripts easily maintain their civilian perspective and, using cell phones and the internet, keep in close communication with their families and friends.

The Lives of Soldiers

It is a fraught task to identify the soldiers' self-image. In the preliterate Russian army—a period of more than 200 years—one is reliant on the mostly unreliable observations of officers and context to draw tentative conclusions. Only with the increase of literacy in the second half of the nineteenth century did the soldiers' voices give insight to their self-image. Under serfdom, his send-off from his town or village, traditionally a drunken affair, was like a funeral or a farewell to a man given a sentence of life at hard labor, so it is doubtful he would see himself as a proud patriot going off to do his duty. It was more like he was being punished, as indeed many were. However, because his social status changed, a soldier did see himself as separate and different from the rest of society. How he might have felt about his distinct status is unknowable. Because the judiciary routinely sentenced men to serve in the army as punishment, it challenged the view that military service was an honorable vocation. For the last 150 years, the insignificant rate of reenlistment indicates that most soldiers have not seen a career in the army as worthwhile and eagerly return to civilian life.

The Soviet regime wanted the men to identify as servants of the people and attach their loyalty to the state. During and after the Second World War (1939–45), the Soviet state elevated the image of the soldier above that of the worker, previously the idol of the October Revolution and the Soviet society. Despite this positive attention, with short, two-year stints of service, conscripts saw their time in the army as brief but unwelcome interruptions of their lives. During the Cold War (1948–91), the Soviet Army grew to more than four million men, conscripting and discharging around a half a million men every six months. The majority of Russian men served in the army between the ages of 20 and 22, making the experience normative and therefore unexceptional.

Following the demise of the Soviet Union, soldiers have been fed a diet of Russian nationalism. Over the course of the 1990s, the army shrank to about 850,000 men and women and began to recruit volunteers on a contract basis. The length of service was reduced first from two years to eighteen months and then to just one year. Although Russian President Boris Yeltsin (1991–99) announced his intent to create an all-volunteer army in the 1990s, it took nearly thirty years for a significant portion of soldiers to be on contract (*kontraktniki*). In 2020, the army claimed 405,000 men (47 percent of manpower) were *kontraktniki*. The growth of contract service did not, however, mean that men's attitude towards service had improved and that the identity of being a soldier became positive. Although contract pay is better than that of conscripts, fewer than half of *kontraktniki* re-enlist, even though they are virtually guaranteed raises and promotions.

Under the old regime, men's self-worth was challenged by regulations that set them lower than even the poorest civilian. Soldiers were allowed to ride only in third- or fourth-class railroad cars. On streetcars they were forbidden to enter the car but had to stand on the platform. Enlisted men were not allowed to smoke on the street, could not dine in nice restaurants or first- and second-class railroad-station buffets. Soldiers were not allowed to sit in the loges or the orchestra of theaters. St. Petersburg was off limits to all soldiers not assigned to the garrison.[1] Soldiers were not allowed freedom of expression, their letters were censored, and reading materials were tightly controlled. All of this changed in the short term with the fall of the monarchy in March 1917. Then, soldiers were given all the rights of citizenship, including freedom of expression and the right to join political parties. These rights only lasted until the end of Russia's Civil War (1918–21), at which time the only acceptable political activities were to join the Bolshevik Party and support its policies. Soldiers regained the right to engage in politics in 1991.

Following the Revolution, soldiers were more likely to have a positive self-image. The Communist Party told the men that they were the guardians of a new progressive order. The Party used the soldiers' time in the service to indoctrinate them in Marxist ideology and to give them an air of self-importance, all in hopes that they would, once discharged, become local leaders back in their factories and villages.[2] After the Second World War and the waning of ideological fervor, peacetime service was seen as something to be endured, not to be looked forward to or to wax nostalgic about afterwards. The reality of daily life in the army during the Cold War made men feel neglected and abused and that their service had been a waste of time.

The Lives of Soldiers

The Quotidian Reality of Service

The historic trend, from the seventeenth to the twenty-first century, is that even when the soldiers had a positive self-image of their service, most entered the service reluctantly, and few chose to stay in the army any longer than required. Among the reasons for the scant volunteerism and lack of reenlistments have been low social status for the enlisted ranks, low pay (until the 2010s), poor food, spartan living conditions, violence at the hands of superiors, violence among soldiers, insignificant veterans' benefits, and an aversion to military life. In sum, daily life in the army is an obstacle preventing most soldiers from investing in the army.

Housing

From Peter I's founding of the army in the late seventeenth century, up to emancipation and the subsequent adoption of the law on universal military obligation, soldiers were quartered among the population for seven or eight months out of the year. They lived in tents in military encampments during the summer months. Soldiers did not expect any better, and it was not much different from the village life they had experienced before conscription. In these conditions, health was poor due to proximity to livestock, an unhygienic environment, and nutrition of indifferent quality and quantity.

In the era of the great reforms, 1856–81, the army high command made major efforts to improve daily life by instituting a massive building program that moved soldiers out of villages and into garrisons with barracks, bathhouses, mess halls, and chapels. This enabled a healthier environment that reduced the peacetime death toll of soldiers. Although the soldiers were away from filthy lice-ridden peasant huts, life in barracks still left much to be desired. Soldiers slept in bunks with straw-filled mattresses but no bed linen. They used their greatcoats for blankets. It was not until 1906 that regiment commanders were required to provide sheets and blankets. Heating the barracks was a hit-or-miss affair dependent on the vigilance of the officers in making firewood available. Communal sleeping quarters meant that sick soldiers would easily spread their illnesses. When command emphasis was slack, barracks fell into disrepair, and hygiene suffered.

Opportunities for entertainment were few. Because soldiers were generally restricted to garrison, boredom was a serious problem. Soldiers were intentionally stationed far from their home districts to discourage desertion and were never granted leave. Naturally, contact with home helped with morale. Private Zakharko, in 1912 wrote that, "Every rifleman loved to talk about his letters and of getting discharged." Zakharko and his draft cohort, who benefited from the progressive reforms following the Revolution of 1905, thought being a soldier was not really that difficult. The hard part was the boredom, loneliness, lack of freedom, and separation from family.[3] In the Putin era, soldiers may choose to be stationed close to home, live off post, and leave the barracks to find entertainment.

Barracks life was not so different during the Soviet period. Soldiers were still restricted to their garrisons unless they were lucky enough to be stationed in a large city such as Leningrad or Moscow. Well-maintained barracks with running water and electricity made life bearable, but there was no guarantee the officers would make sure the facilities were kept up. The Ministry of Defense consistently allocated insufficient funds for garrison maintenance, and supplies were routinely misappropriated by senior officers. Today, life in barracks varies depending on the conscientiousness of the commanders. Ill-health or death is likely when officers misappropriate funds intended for upkeep and maintenance. In 2015, a dilapidated barracks in Omsk collapsed, killing twenty-three soldiers because the officers did not maintain the building. Although men use cell phones to keep in touch with family and friends, thus mitigating their isolation, life remains spartan and devoid of amenities, unless soldiers pay for them out of their own pockets.

Pay

Conscript soldiers' pay had been nominal from Peter I (1696–1721) to Putin. The Russian army has exhibited a historic aversion to paying conscripts decent wages, usually, since the seventeenth century, only kopeks or a few rubles a month. The operating assumption is that the men owe the state their service, but the state does not owe them living wages. This view was clearly articulated by a general in 1904—and still holds true among officers to this day—who told American politician Alfred Beveridge:

> We think it is a mistake to pay soldiers. It puts the military service of the country on a mercenary basis. The theory should be that every man should be prepared to give not only three or four years of service, but his life, if need be, to his country; but the idea of pay debases the spirit of this service.[4]

The hypocrisy of this position is obvious as officers have habitually whined about their wages being insufficient. The army claims to provide the soldier with everything he needs in the way of food, clothing, and shelter, thus obviating the need for soldiers to have money but ignores the human desire for personal items and the need for entertainment. Soldiers of the Imperial Russian Army, paid less than thirty-three rubles annually, usually had the opportunity to work for pay in the civilian economy for several months during the year. Officers arranged the work with the understanding that some of the proceeds were for the use of the regiment, with the soldiers keeping the rest. In the Soviet era, soldiers were used as labor on construction projects and to help collective farmers during the sowing and harvest, but for the benefit of the state not themselves or the army.

Red Army soldiers, like their imperial precedents, were paid a pittance. Soldiers earned the equivalent of $5 per month, sergeants $15, compared to the average worker who earned $160. In the Putin era, *kontraktniki* earned relatively decent wages. As recently as 2020, monthly wages amounted to the equivalent of $600, enough to cover soldiers' basic needs and desires. Conscripts, however, are still miserably paid, with monthly pay the equivalent of just $17.05, which is entirely inadequate and insulting considering that, in 2022, a teenager working in a Moscow McDonald's restaurant earned $420 a month for a thirty-five-hour work week.

Social History of the Russians and Their Army

Nutrition

Although the army does provide housing and uniforms, it rarely adequately feeds the men. For nearly 300 years, when a regiment was quartered on the population, tea, bread, and buckwheat groats generally constituted the soldiers' daily fare. Before the post-1905 reforms, the men usually received only bread for breakfast. For lunch, the men got cabbage soup or soup prepared with one-quarter pound of meat, or porridge. Sometimes, potato soup with fish was added to the mix. When they could, soldiers supplemented their diet with bread purchased out of pocket. For dinner, they were fed porridge and salami or gruel. On special regimental or religious holidays, the soldiers were given a cup of vodka or beer, perogi, half a pound of meat, and assorted pastries.[5] Regiments occasionally purchased additional food with specially designated funds called "soup money." Meat appeared on the menu irregularly and was usually purchased by regiments on the hoof. Until soldiers were billeted in garrisons with mess halls, they divided themselves into small groups called *artels* and cooked their food themselves.[6] When regiments were in settled quarters, most established farms with gardens and livestock. Even with these gardens, soldiers asked their families to send money so they could buy more food. Those families that did send money to their sons usually did not have much to give.[7]

Senior officers were generally dismissive of soldiers' complaints about the poor quality and insufficient quantity of food. General Anton Denikin, typical of tsarist generals, believed that, "In terms of calories and suitability, the food was entirely adequate and in any case, was more nourishing than the food which the peasants had at home."[8] Despite the officers' opinion that the men were well fed, dissatisfaction about food, in addition to many other quality-of-life issues, was a major cause of disobedience during the Revolution of 1905 and February Revolution in 1917 (Figure 1.1).

After the October Revolution in 1917, the new Red Army intended to feed the soldiers well but did not always succeed. Mess hall operations and food procurement became centralized at division level. During the famine of 1932–33, when millions of Soviet citizens

The Lives of Soldiers

Figure 1.1 Days of revolution—troops on the Liteinyi Prospect. Saint Petersburg, Soviet Union Russia, 1917. Photograph. https://www.loc.gov/item/2009631819/.

starved to death, the army reestablished regimental farms, which it maintained into the 1990s. Soldiers, who were supposed to be fed 4,112 calories per day, complained during the Cold War years about both the monotony and quality of mess hall fare, which was in many ways a reflection of the food situation throughout the USSR, though exacerbated by corruption among supply officers. Then, like their counterparts in the tsarist army and like their successors today, underpaid conscripts appealed to their families for money to augment the official rations.

Soldiers' Health

For more than two hundred years, the famous Thomas Hobbes quote—"the life of man, solitary, poor, nasty, brutish, and short"—applied not only to the Russian peasant but also to the soldier. From 1826 to 1856, the official annual death rate among soldiers in peacetime was 37.4 per 1,000 that is likely lower than reality due to intentional under-reporting by commanders who stood to gain by having inflated rosters. In the same years, in the French, Prussian, and Austrian armies, the death rate was 20 per 1,000. In that time frame, a total of 1,028,650 Russian soldiers died from sickness, disease, accidents, and other non-combat-related causes—more than 34,000 per year. Most deaths resulted from epidemics, tainted food, insufficient nutrition, and brutality. In the early 1870s, for example, of every 1,000 soldiers in the St. Petersburg Military District—most of whom lived in barracks—every year, 700 became ill enough to need medical treatment, and of these, at least forty would die. Seldom mentioned in official reports were the numerous cases of suicide.[9]

During the reform era, the modest expansion of military medical services and shorter terms of service improved life expectancy during peacetime. As early as 1870, the average annual death rate had been nearly halved to 19.2 per thousand men. The 1880s' barracks-building program, the reduced use of corporal punishment, and the waning of interpersonal violence against soldiers by superiors further lowered the annual peacetime death rate to 5.4 per thousand in 1894.[10] Statistics for health and death rates during the Soviet era are unavailable, but anecdotal evidence suggests that life in the army was about as healthy as it was in civilian life. The availability of medical care steadily expanded. Safe drinking water, indoor plumbing, and attention to personal hygiene created conditions for a healthier environment. The Ministry of Defense, in 2014, claimed to have made a concerted effort to improve the health of soldiers by heating the barracks, installing washing machines and shower facilities, and requiring troops to bathe more than once a week.

Even as the army improved the health of soldiers in the late nineteenth century, it degraded the men's health through the daily allocation of vodka at the evening meal. The result of the widespread use of alcohol in the Imperial Russian Army was that, by the 1890s, alcohol poisoning was estimated to cause at least 10 percent of all deaths.[11] Before the emancipation and subsequent reforms, soldiers' access to alcohol was haphazard. Mostly they bought or bargained with peasants for moonshine (*samogon*). Some officers blamed peer pressure for alcohol abuse. Others blamed boredom and the lack of entertainment and recreational opportunities. Alcohol abuse often led to dereliction of duty or crimes and misdemeanors that ranged from absence without leave, waste or destruction of property, general dissipation, and to more serious crimes such as injurious assaults and murder.[12]

The Bolsheviks were keenly aware of the scourge of alcoholism and so abolished the vodka ration and prohibited the sale of alcohol on Red Army bases. Soviet Army regulations forbade alcohol consumption by soldiers on and off duty. The most significant exception to this rule was made during the Second World War. Then, 100 grams of vodka per soldier per day were authorized for frontline troops. After the war, the ban on alcohol on military bases and its use by soldiers was probably the most flaunted regulation in the Soviet Army. Alcohol abuse became tolerated as a cultural norm in the military. One lieutenant, interviewed in 1982, said: "Everybody drinks all the time."[13] In the early 1980s, 20 percent of armed forces personnel were estimated to be chronic alcoholics and another 30–35 percent heavy drinkers.

Conscripts usually obtained alcohol through selling or bartering their military equipment and clothing, theft, robbing liquor stores or wine shops, or with money sent from home. Soldiers mostly consumed alcohol in drinking bouts rather than on a daily basis. The result was that every year hundreds of soldiers died or went blind from alcohol poisoning and or fatal accidents involving firearms, vehicles, and aircraft. The reasons Soviet soldiers drank were nearly identical to those of the Imperial Russian Army soldier: homesickness, isolation, boredom, and lack of healthy diversions.[14] The abuse of alcohol and the consequent effects continue in the Army of the Russian Federation. Alcohol is readily available in stores and drinking establishments near military bases.

Training and Indoctrination

From the Peter I to Putin, the Russian soldier has been given his individual basic training in his regiment at the hands of his sergeants. Under the old regime, when conscripts reported for duty in the late fall, sergeants trained them during the winter months. With the Soviet and current practice of conscripts reporting twice a year, basic training is for the first two to three months of their service. Basic training consists of learning how to march, how to wear the uniform, how to salute, whom to salute, how to address officers, and all the regulations pertinent to his branch of service. Marksmanship with small arms and the use of the bayonet and hand grenades are also part of basic training. Training on heavy weapons and specialized equipment follows basic training. Finally, until nearly the twentieth century, training to fight as part of a unit, from the squad to battalion, was reserved for the annual summer camp.

Part of a soldier's training is being indoctrinated into the military ethos. To this end, Russian soldiers, from Peter I to Nicholas II (1894–1917), swore loyalty to the person of the sovereign and were taught the catechism of the soldier. The catechism informed the soldier that he served the tsar, not the nation. The answer to the question "What is a soldier?" was, "A soldier is a servant of the Sovereign and the Fatherland and defends them from foreign and domestic enemies." The concept of duty was used to support the idea of dying for the tsar. When asked, "What is a sense of military duty?" the soldier was to answer: "The sense of duty is that sense which enables a man to overcome the fear of death ... 'it is better to die than fail one's duty, or one's oath.'"[15] The sanctity of military regulations and unquestioning obedience to orders are still considered fundamental to the education of Russian soldiers.

After the October Revolution of 1917, soldiers no longer memorized a catechism but swore their loyalty to the Soviet state. In the oath of allegiance, made at a solemn ceremony at the completion of basic training, he vowed "to be an honest, brave, disciplined and vigilant fighter, to guard strictly all military and state secrets, to obey implicitly all army regulations and orders of my commanders, commissars and superiors." He promised to be conscientious in his duties and "to be true to my People, my Soviet Motherland, and the Workers' and Peasants' Government to my last breath." Finally, he promised "to defend her courageously, skillfully, creditably and honorably," at the cost of his life to defeat the enemy. Soldiers of the Russian Federation vow to obey military regulations, orders of officers, and to perform

Figure 1.2 Soldier of the Army of the Russian Federation taking the oath of service. iStock photos.

their military duties "with dignity, courageously defend the freedom, independence and constitutional order of Russia, the people and the Motherland" (Figure 1.2).

The tsarist army also employed the Russian Orthodox Church to shape soldiers' attitudes and control their behavior. The tsar and officers put great store in the power of religion and the clergy to put the fear of God into the men and to instill loyalty to the tsar and autocracy. The daily schedule included an evening Bible lesson, also known as an "instructive talk," led by the regiment's priest, a deacon or an NCO. Soldiers were required to recite a special prayer for the tsar. The fifth commandment to honor one's mother and father was used to reinforce the soldiers' duty to obey their superiors, invoking the sense that the army was a family, the officers were the parents and soldiers the children.[16] Until 1906, attending religious services was mandatory for Orthodox Christians if a priest was available.

The Red Army, obviously, dispensed with priests and religion and instead employed commissars to inculcate a sense of duty to the new regime and its revolutionary program. Every company-sized unit had a political officer, and each battalion and higher unit had a commissar assigned to the Main Military Political Administration (GlavPUR), which answered to the Communist Party rather than to the military chain of command. Political instruction was held once a week. Initially, the goal was to teach Marxism to the soldiers, but, because of the ignorance of the instructors and soldiers alike, political instruction devolved into information sessions about the Party's take on the news of the day. Communism's demise saw the abolition of GlavPUR.

Putin revived religion in the Russian army as part of his nationalist agenda. In 2009, he coopted the Russian Orthodox Church to instill national patriotic values in the same manner as had the Imperial Russian Army. The army hired hundreds of Orthodox priests and in 2020 built a gigantic cathedral dedicated to the Russian army. To augment the work of the priests, in 2019, on Putin's instruction, the army reintroduced the position of political officer at the battalion and regiment levels. Their job, like that of the communist political officer, is to feed soldiers the official version of events, monitor political attitudes, act as morale officer, and to serve as the commander's liaison with the soldiers' families.

Soldiers and Superiors

Until the emancipation of the serfs in 1861, serfs sent to the army were under no illusion that they would be treated any differently by their noble officers and the NCOs than they were by their landowners or their stewards or bailiffs. Superiors' treatment of subordinates was characterized by the arbitrary use of physical violence, lack of legal protections, and judicial punishments that soldiers could not appeal. Regiment commanders, like serf owners, acted as prosecutor, judge, and jury, dispensing corporal punishment for crimes or violations of regulations in a range of severity from a few dozen to several hundred lashes with the knout or birch rod or order the running of the gauntlet—virtually a death sentence. Soldiers viewed their officers in the same negative light as they viewed their landowners. As on a landed estate, slaps, punches, and kicks from irate superiors were a part of daily life. Officers and NCOs used the words "train" and "beat" interchangeably. This was all justified by the officers, many from serf-owing families, because socially inferior soldiers, like serfs, were considered stupid, ignorant, and unwilling to do more than they were forced to do. Soldiers could and did complain about unfair treatment on an individual basis. How that turned out was completely dependent on the personality of the commander. When soldiers complained in groups, it was considered a collective act of disobedience bordering on mutiny and was punished harshly.

As a reminder of their social inferiority, soldiers were required to address their officers not by their rank but with reference to their social standing. Ensigns, lieutenants, and captains were addressed as "Your Nobility." Lieutenant-colonels and colonels as "Your High Nobility." Major-generals and lieutenant-generals were greeted with "Your Excellency," and higher-ranking generals were "Your High Excellency." Soldiers always addressed officers with the formal "*vy*," but officers condescended by speaking to soldiers with the familiar "*ty*." When greeting his troops, the commander addressed them with "Hello, children!" The soldiers, standing at attention, responded in unison "Good health, your excellency!" or alternatively "Happy to serve, your excellency!" or whatever the appropriate appellation might be.[17]

The February 1917 Revolution put an end to the paternalistic and social basis of the officer-enlisted relationship. The new Red Army, led overwhelmingly by commoners, encouraged soldiers to see their officers as comrades who just happened to hold a superior military position. The comradely approach was dispensed with during the Second World War, and thereafter a strict rank-based hierarchical relation was imposed. With it, the adversarial relationship resumed and continued into the modern Russian army.

Soldiers' Expectation Post-Emancipation

The emancipation created a new generation of soldiers and marked a historical shift in how soldiers expected to be treated. The failure of the soldiers' expectations of humane treatment to be met eventually resulted in the mutinies of 1905–06 and the February Revolution.

Because the culture of violence against soldiers by officers and NCOs proved deeply entrenched, better treatment at the hands of their officers was slow in coming despite official policy discouraging violence. Soldiers' hopes and expectations rose when a raft of reforms in the 1860s and 1870s gave the soldiers legal rights against the arbitrary power of commanders and limited the use of corporal punishment. Physical violence against soldiers was officially proscribed but enforcement was lax. Running the gauntlet and the use of the knout were abolished, and the system of military tribunals was regularized.

Alexander II supported reformist officers who wanted to moderate, if not eliminate, corporal punishment in the armed forces, arguing that emancipation had created a new social and legal status for the peasantry, thus obviating the suitability of a punitive code based on serfdom. It needed to be abandoned in favor of one appropriate for men in a free society. In 1863, corporal punishment was banned as the predominant form of punishment in the armed forces. In practice, this ban just reduced the frequency of its use. Until then, corporal punishment was the basis of all punishment in Russian law. The reformers' intent was to eventually eliminate the use of the rod and to punish serious crime with imprisonment.

From the 1870s onward, the army built guardhouses for short-term incarceration and organized disciplinary battalions for longer periods. In general, the spirit of the reformers was to replace punishment with rehabilitation. Discipline in disciplinary battalions was strict but bearable. Soldiers had a set routine of training, physical exercise, and work, but also basic education classes for reading, writing, and arithmetic. Initially, the Red Army did away with such units but restored them in 1939. Disciplinary battalions continue to be used in the Army of the Russian Federation in which conditions, depending on the commander, sometimes degenerate into hell on earth with sadistic treatment of soldiers by officers and guards. Hazing among prisoners sinks to depraved levels of torture and sexual abuse.[18]

Despite the slow improvement in the quality of life in the army after emancipation, the hundreds of mutinies during the Revolution of 1905 indicate that soldiers expected better, which put them at odds with their officers, who believed they were getting what they deserved.

The Lives of Soldiers

Mutinous soldiers invariably presented lists of demands to the regiment commander. Over half of all lists included shorter terms of service and better treatment of enlisted men by officers and NCOs. Some even demanded that abusive officers and NCOs be removed from their unit. There were demands to make the system of military justice fairer and to reduce the disciplinary powers of officers. Many soldiers demanded an end to physical abuse disguised as disciplinary punishment. Soldiers demanded higher pay to meet their daily needs. Some mutineers made demands for a shorter workday, more free time, and the right to leave the garrison during off-duty hours. Soldiers also demanded better maintenance of the barracks to make them more sanitary and healthier. There were demands for bathhouses and the opportunity to bathe weekly. Over half of all soldiers' demands included more and better food. Soldiers wanted linens for the barracks, better boots, and more issues of uniforms; they especially desired warm uniforms for the winter. Nearly 20 percent of the lists included demands for home leave at some time during a man's enlistment. Soldiers also wanted unit libraries and newspaper subscriptions.[19]

The constitutional government brought about by the Revolution of 1905 dramatically improved conditions for soldiers and raised expectations of yet better treatment. Terms of service were cut in half from six to three years. Soldiers were issued bed linens, blankets, and more uniforms, pay was raised but only marginally, more food was promised, and bath houses were built. Most important, the army issued regulations forbidding officers and NCOs from physically abusing their men.

Russians' expectations of higher quality of life in the army rose further in the early Soviet period. Soldiers saw themselves as citizens with rights equal to their superiors and deserving of respect. Until the outbreak of the Second World War, the army, watched over by GlavPUR, worked diligently to eradicate the physical abuse of soldiers and demeaning behavior by superiors. Due largely to budgetary constraints, the quality of food, housing, and uniforms was low but not bad. Pay was still negligible (Figure 1.3).

During the Second World War, treatment of soldiers deteriorated. Physical abuse by officers and NCOs began to creep back into

Social History of the Russians and Their Army

Figure 1.3 Red Army soldiers in the USSR (Union of Soviet Socialist Republics). Russian Federation, 1941? Photograph. https://www.loc.gov/item/2017824539/.

superior-subordinate relations. After the war, and into the post-Soviet era, slapping and punching of soldiers by superiors, while officially banned, unofficially has been tolerated. Such treatment adds to the poor reputation of the army in Russian society. Soldiers in the twenty-first century desire but are under no illusions that they will be treated any better than their Imperial and Soviet Army predecessors because they have no faith in the army to create a better environment.

Orthodoxy, Autocracy, Nationality

Historically, the experience of service has varied according to a soldier's class, race, religion, nationality, and ethnicity. For nearly the entirety of Russian military history, the majority of soldiers have come from the peasantry, so the Russian peasant has been represented as the typical soldier. Soldiers from other demographics have been measured against him and his experience. In the 2020s, the rural poor still are more likely to be drafted or to take a contract than men from urban areas. Men from affluent or politically connected families have always easily avoided service. Those men coming from well-educated and well-off families who have found themselves in uniform typically serve only brief stints—the Law on Universal Military Obligation of 1874 stipulated shorter terms of service based on the level of education to as few as twelve months for college-educated males. In the Soviet period, it could be as few as six months. Russians were more likely than other nationalities to have the economic and educational wherewithal to secure deferments or shorter terms of service. Educated men were more likely to be assigned to positions that required literacy and higher mathematic skills, such as clerks, or any technical jobs than to be sent to the infantry.

As poorly as Russian soldiers were treated, they still fared better than their counterparts from all the other nationalities. Tsar Nicholas I (1825–55), established the watchwords "Orthodoxy, Autocracy, Nationality" to define his regime's ideals. The ideal subject was of the Russian Orthodox faith, supported autocracy as the natural political order, and believed that Russians were the superior nationality and had the superior culture. The millions in the empire who were neither Orthodox nor Russian were encouraged to convert and to adopt the language and cultural norms of Russians. Those who clung to alternative identities or political outlooks were considered lesser subjects and held suspect. Under Alexander III (1881–94), the regime launched a Russification program to suppress non-Russian languages, cultures, and religions and to encourage the "others" in the empire to be like Russians. This sometimes had the opposite effect—it magnified the non-Russians' attachment to their "other" identity.

Ethnic minorities were more likely to be assigned the dirtiest, most unpleasant tasks and suffer more brutal physical punishments than Russians. Non-Russian Slavs, particularly Ukrainians and Belarusians, were next in the hierarchy of privilege and treatment and were officially referred to as "little brother Slavs." It was a given that Slavs (other than Poles) were of the Russian Orthodox faith. Lower on the scale of ideal soldiers were Catholics (Poles and Lithuanians), then Lutherans (Estonians, Latvians, Finns, and Germans). Non-Slavs—among them Jews, Muslim Caucasians, and Central Asians—were actively discriminated against and treated as lesser people. Although officially condemned, racial animosities did not disappear with the Bolshevik Revolution but carried over into the Red Army and beyond. The Army of the Russian Federation under Putin again promoted Russian nationality and Russian Orthodoxy as the ideal and authoritarian politics as best for Russia. The promotion of Orthodoxy by Putin increased the tension between Russians and Muslims—tension that frequently manifests in violence between soldiers and discrimination by officers, especially those who served in the Chechen wars.[20]

Not only race and religion, but nationality and ethnicity determined the level of consideration and treatment meted out to subordinates by superiors and the military system. The 1874 Law on Universal Military Obligation exempted Muslims of the Caucasus, Finns, peoples of the northern territories, the non-Russian peoples of Turkestan, Russia's Far East, and the remote parts of Siberia. However, after much debate, Jews were included in the draft pool. The army high command secretly decreed that every regiment should be at least 75 percent "Russian" (Russian, Belorussian, and Ukrainian). Poles, soldiers from the Baltics, and other nationalities were spread out to keep them isolated to inhibit rebellion. The Soviet Army and the Army of the Russian Federation continued this practice. In the Soviet period, all men, regardless of race or ethnicity, were subject to conscription, and the army became much more multi-ethnic, though Slavs still predominated. With the collapse of the USSR, the new Russian army became more homogeneous, with far fewer non-Slavs and non-Russians to draw on for military service.

Soldiers' Interpersonal Relations

Ethnically Russian soldiers, encouraged by the official position that they are superior, typically have victimized and discriminated against non-Russian soldiers. Since 1875, racist attitudes toward Jews,

The Lives of Soldiers

Caucasians, and Central Asians, combined with religious bigotry and dismissive attitudes to other national minorities, have divided soldiers against each other and hindered unit cohesion. Anti-Semitism, rife in Russian society, was certainly not discouraged in the imperial army, and treating Jews with respect and dignity was frowned upon. Officers in the imperial army generally saw Jews as a subversive element, disloyal and prone to socialism, and blamed them for political unrest. Violence against Jews by soldiers typically went unpunished.

National minorities were held to be inferior and suspect. During the First World War, an Estonian soldier, Samuel Kütman, asserted, "It should be said in that regard to Russians, who lack education, they are indeed nasty people, and they take it out most of all on the Estonian people." Another Estonian, Adolf-Arthur Kuldkep, considered deserting because of maltreatment at the hands of Russian soldiers, whom he referred to as "idiots."[21] Russian soldiers had pejorative names for all minorities and used them freely. Their relations were often guided by ethnic stereotyping. They saw Balts as obsessed with national liberation, but cultured, quiet, and decent. Central Asians were considered primitive, meek, and lazy. Soldiers from the Caucasus produced the strongest emotional reactions among Russians, ranging from fascination to fear, because they were believed to be clannish and explosively dauntless.[22]

The Red Army declared all its citizens to be equal and officially banned discrimination. Anti-Semitism was forbidden. With command emphasis, the communist regime was largely able to suppress overt manifestations of inter-ethnic strife but failed to eliminate deep-seated, culturally based animosities among the men. In Putin's Russia, non-Russians are again held suspect and discriminated against. The stereotypes and prejudices of the imperial period persist to this day.

Hazing

By far most deleterious to the public perception of the army and soldiers' quality of life is the practice of hazing (*dedovshchina*), a phenomenon traced to the 1960s. *Dedovshchina* means rule of the grandfathers, which coincided with the changes in the conscription system enacted in the 1960s, in which the army switched from annual to a semi-annual conscription. This led to constant turnover of personnel. Every six months a new cohort arrived, and the oldest one was discharged. The oldest cohort was made up of the "grandfathers" (*dedy*), who had six months left in the army. The *dedy* were divided between the *stariki*, who have six months of service remaining, and the *dembels* with only three months left until discharge. Soldiers who were between the most junior and senior were called "skulls." Skulls generally left the new soldiers alone and did not challenge senior soldiers while they waited for their turn to become *stariki*. The men in their first six months of service were called "spirits" and were the victims of the *stariki's* hazing, which mostly took the form of stealing the new recruits' possessions, uniforms, and money, and of having them do all the menial chores assigned to the *stariki*, accompanied by physical violence if the victim resisted. In extreme cases, hazing included extortion, homosexual rape, and murder. "Grandfathers" ganged up on and beat soldiers who resisted. Regardless of what the senior soldiers did, most new soldiers went along with it because they saw no other alternative.

From the 2000s onward, *kontraktniki* are the "grandfathers," and all conscripts, no matter what month of service they are in, are targets. Exactly how and why hazing became a feature of military service is still debated, but there's no question that its existence further alienates many soldiers from the army and deters volunteers. In 2009, 70 percent of young men polled reported that *dedovshchina* was the reason they did not want to serve in the army.

Without emphasis from the very top of the government and the army, change is highly unlikely. In March 2011, the Minister of Defense, Anatoly Serdiukov, addressed the personnel of the Ministry of Defense, and rather than offering solutions to hazing, accepted its inevitability, saying: "It is not possible to reduce the level of offenses caused by hazing of military personnel. The reason for this is the increase in the number of recruits over the past two years, more than twice, as well as serious omissions in the work of individual commanders." He offered the non-solution that "the personal responsibility of commanders and chiefs for ensuring military discipline has been increased."²³ President Medvedev, at the same meeting, reiterated Serdiukov's statement. Either they had no idea how to intervene or were unwilling to force the necessary changes.

If the army is a reflection of society, then the officers who blame society for *dedovshchina*, may not be entirely off the mark. Contemporary Russian sociologists believe that Russia's prison culture permeates Russian society and by extension affects the army. One sociological study has shown that, like soldiers in the army, prisoners in Russia divide themselves into formal and informal categories. There are three basic groups: *blatnye* (thieves) are the elite prisoners who make the rules and enforce the norms of this society; *muzhiki* (ordinary guys) are the middle tier of prisoners who strive to maintain their autonomy through labor; and the *shesterki* (sixes, because there are six subcategories in this category) who are prisoners beholden to and abused by the *blatnye*. Rather than guards maintaining order among prisoners, the prison administration relies on prisoners, called *smotriashchy* (watchers), who are drawn from the *blatnye*. Sociologist Anton Oleinik notes that there are similarities between the prison community and broader Russian society. He argues that everyday Russian life is filled with "elements typical of the socio-psychological makeup of the prison inmate" and that people—to include President Putin—commonly use prison slang in everyday speech. Oleinik says the inmate's creed of "no trust, no fear, no questions" is reflected in civil society's "every man for himself" attitude.²⁴ This attitude is referenced constantly by former soldiers. A sad, if not terrible, irony is that after the October Revolution, the Bolsheviks characterized service in the old army as a prison sentence to contrast it to the humane and honorable service the Red Army promised, but by the end of the Soviet era, the prison analogy was more apt than ever.

The violent, tough-guy culture of street gangs, often referenced by Putin, also permeates society and the military. In the two generations of Russian males who have come of age since the 1980s, one in four has been incarcerated, meaning that the culture of street violence meshes with that of prison culture. Human rights activist Valery Abramkin notes that "prison culture, with its romanticized image of criminal outlaws, songs and slang, has always been within easy reach in working-class city quarters. The street absorbed this culture like a sponge, and successive generations of Russian men learned the language that is now often heard from public tribunes."[25] The street toughs' predilection for violence as part of their sense of masculinity has contributed, according to the Violent Societies Index, to Russia being ranked among the top ten most violent societies in the 1990s and the 2000s.[26] The army's recruiting ads appeal to the street gangster image as the personification of warrior masculinity. With urban poor men and men with criminal records making up a sizeable portion of draftees and *kontraktniki*, it is no wonder that without close oversight by officers, barracks can be violent, dangerous, and virtually lawless places. Like prison wardens and guards, officers and political leaders mostly ignore the violence among their charges.

Soldiers' response to *dedovshchina* varies. Some believe that it is a positive toughening-up process and claim to feel more "manly" after their service for having had the experience. Others feel anger, fear, and hatred. A few fight back. Suicides are not uncommon. Some "grandfathers" refrain from harassing younger soldiers but seldom speak up against abuse. Those who see it as a positive process also view it as a failure on the part of the officers to lead and maintain discipline. One veteran, when interviewed years after his service, credited *dedovshchina* with turning him into a soldier, saying, "I don't support *dedovshchina*, but when I served, I thought it was necessary. It maintained order." He reflected that "*dedovshchina* disciplines you, without doubt."[27]

Dedovshchina reinforces the feeling in Russian society that military service is not only undesirable and to be avoided but also delegitimizes the state's right to demand universal military service. Gorbachev's *glasnost* enabled the broad public to learn about the physical brutality (although it was well known among families of soldiers) in the army, which led Liubov Lymar to found a mass movement, the Committee of Soldiers Mothers (CSM) in 1989 to protest the maltreatment of their sons in the army, after her own son, Oleg, was found dead with his tongue cut out in 1988 (Figure 1.4). The emergence of the CSM was a watershed moment in Russian history in that it asserted the right

The Lives of Soldiers

Figure 1.4 An action organized by the Latvian Women's League at the Freedom Monument in Riga, 1989. Photographer Ģirts Ozoliņš, with the permission of the Latvian Museum of Occupation.

of citizens to organize and to hold the government accountable. The violence endemic to the barracks calls into question the character-building claims of the army in the face of the real trauma and psychological damage done to some recruits that leads to suicide and murder.[28] One mother, whose son received a draft notice during the first Chechen War, had this to say when asked if she would let her son report for duty:

> Never! No one cares that my eldest boy was bullied quite unmercifully in the army and returned home not entirely in his right mind. I'm the one that's bringing him round, and healing his nerves and his mind, which have been unbalanced by that army for many years to come. The State has done nothing to treat him. So now they want my next son? Not for anything in this world.[29]

The CSM confronted military authorities at all levels, from regiments to the Ministry of Defense. Originally created to protest hazing, it soon launched activities geared to the defense of soldiers' rights in general. After the disintegration of the USSR, the committee changed its title to the Union of Committees of Soldiers' Mothers of Russia (UCSMR) and established branches throughout the Russian Federation. They identified themselves as a nongovernmental human rights organization (NGO). Using funds solicited from its members and the public, the UCSMR established rehabilitation centers for soldiers who left the army for health reasons, and to lobby legislators for change. In the 1990s, it expanded its efforts to include the organization of human rights education for conscripts, their parents, and wives. It taught women how to make individual complaints concerning human rights violations against their sons or husbands. Through local chapters, it instituted regular inspections of military units and organized public protests. At the national level, with the assistance of sympathetic law makers, the UCSMR lobbied for laws requiring the Ministry of Defense to the release of statistics on deaths in the army, to investigate all cases of death in peacetime, and for the guilty to be punished; to establish independent juries and commissions to investigate human rights violations in the army; to grant amnesty for soldiers who deserted out of fear for their health or lives; to introduce compensation for relatives in cases of soldiers' deaths; and to improve living conditions of the rank and file. The ultimate goal of the mothers was to establish civilian control over the armed forces to protect the human rights of soldiers.[30]

Mothers, wives, and anyone with a relative in the service, identified with the UCSMR and was liable to complain to the authorities about the treatment of their menfolk. In the first four months of 2022, Russians sent 8,041 complaints about the Ministry of Defense to the Presidential Administration—more than in any year since 2016. Until the beginning of the war against Ukraine in February 2022, the top issues generating complaints were military housing, pensions, awards, military burials, and contract service.[31] These complaints are in a tradition of seeking redress by appealing to the head of state, reaching back to at least the eighteenth century. In the first three months after the Russian invasion of Ukraine, between February and May 2022, Russians sent more than 15,000 inquiries about their sons' whereabouts and welfare to the UCSMR, mostly after having first gotten no answers from the army.

The inexplicable failure and lack of interest on the part of the military to improve the lot of the Russian soldier is the key to understanding the rift between the Russian people and their army. It keeps the populace from fully embracing the military and honoring military service as a worthy experience.

CHAPTER 2
TO SERVE OR NOT TO SERVE

From Peter I's establishment of a regular army in the 1690s to this day, one can characterize Russians' dominant emotion at the prospect of being forced to perform military service as one of dread. In 2012, the Russian Ministry of Defense estimated that 200,000 men had evaded the draft and 244,000 more in 2013.[1] While the availability of statistics on draft evasion is a recent development, the desire to evade military service is as old as the Russian army. Since the reign of Peter I, the lower classes and ethnic minorities have viewed military service negatively. The reasons remain unchanged: low pay, brutal and uncaring treatment by superiors, unhealthy and substandard housing, insufficient and unappealing food, lack of societal appreciation for their service, few veterans' benefits, and the simple fact that military service does not appeal to many people. Only in the 2010s, when contract service paid a living wage, did people, especially youth from impoverished backgrounds, begin to consider military service more positively. Until then, there had been a near universal desire to avoid service in the ranks. This chapter argues that there is an almost instinctive aversion in Russian society to serve in the Russian military.

According to historian Elise Wirtschafter, referring to the pre-emancipation era, "Of all the obligations imposed on the poll-tax population, none was more terrible or feared than military service."[2] Fear was experienced not only by the men dispatched for service, but also by their families. For nearly 225 years, soldiers had little or no hope of ever coming home. Tsar Michael mandated lifelong conscripted service beginning in 1631, which remained in effect until Catherine II reduced it to twenty-five years in 1793. Forty-one years later, Nicholas I set active service at twenty years followed by five in reserve. During the 1840s and 1850s, regiment commanders were authorized to furlough soldiers with unblemished records after fifteen years in the ranks. In the aftermath of the Crimean War, in advance of anticipated reforms, the term of service was reduced to ten years and then six. In the decades following the emancipation, Minister of War General Dmitrii Miliutin enacted reforms that, in 1874, fixed the maximum term of service at six years, with allowance for shorter terms based on levels of education. He also raised the draft age from seventeen years (set by Catherine II, previously it was fifteen) to twenty-one. The government further reduced the terms of service to just three years in the aftermath of the 1905 Revolution. During the Soviet period, between 1923 and 1939, conscripts served for only two years, but this was raised to three years in 1940, where it stayed until 1967, when it was again reduced to two years. In the immediate post-Soviet period, in the 1990s, the term was reduced to eighteen months and in the 2000s to just one year of active service. Soldiers could also volunteer to serve on three-year contracts.

Military service and its effects touched and continue to touch the lives of untold millions of Russians and other peoples of the Russian Empire, Soviet Union, and contemporary Russia. A very rough estimate is that between the years 1700 and 2020, approximately 170 million men and women served in the military, the majority of them (148 million) in the twentieth century. Until 2010, recruitment to the army was based on conscription, though in peacetime there was always a trickle of volunteers, which sometimes increased during wartime. In 2010, recruiting combined conscription and voluntarism. Conscription, and service in general, stands as a regular feature of Russian life, though unevenly experienced on the bases of social class, race, ethnicity, nationality, religion, and income. Until 1875, not every year saw a call for recruits. During wartime, several waves of conscription could be conducted in one year. For example, during the 1700s, there were seventy-two call ups of draftees; between 1800 and 1874, there were seventy-three, with four years having no recruitment. The Law on Universal Military Obligation of 1874 established conscription as a regular, annual event. Annual recruitment remained in effect until the 1967 Law on Universal Military Service transformed it into a bi-annual event, which continues to this day.

Draft Selection and Avoidance

Under serfdom, families feared the loss of an able-bodied male largely because, as an agrarian economy, the labor power of male family members was essential for survival. Because of the potentially catastrophic consequences of losing a man to the army, families did what they could to prevent their men from being taken. In the imperial period, self-interest divided the village community; those who eventually gave up a son to the army saw themselves as losers in the contest for economic survival. The normal system of conscription, not enshrined into law until 1830, was called the "line system" (*ocherednaia sistema*), meaning the first in line to give a recruit were large families, and the last in line were small families. In 1847, an additional law exempted families that had fewer than three men between the ages of twenty and thirty-five from providing a recruit.[3]

Communes did not stick strictly to this scheme and worked to preserve viable families at the expense of those considered weak and unproductive, and to rid the commune of ne'er do wells, drunks, troublemakers, and the unproductive who had accumulated rent arrears to the landowner (which the rest of the commune had to cover). Communes often combined the line system with a lottery in which larger families put in more names and smaller families fewer or none. Peasants followed the guiding principles of survival of the village and fairness, in that order, to govern selection. In 1838, the government mandated that state serfs use only the lottery system but stipulated that a man's name had to go into the lottery only once in his lifetime, and if not drawn, he was thereafter exempt from conscription.[4] Sometimes, heads of household unfairly attempted to protect their sons from the draft through bribery, to the ire of their fellow villagers. The peasants sent the list of those selected to the serf owner or local authority for approval.[5] For the duration of the imperial period, no matter how the selection was conducted, peasants and townspeople—with some justification—universally saw the outcome as inequitably in favor of the wealthier in their communities.

There were those in the army who objected to the methods town councils, villages, and landowners used to select conscripts because so many undesirable men ended up in the army. One of Paul I's generals warned him in the 1790s that, because the army had become the dumping ground for social outcasts and criminals, "the army was made up of 'most villainous and mutinous' people."[6] Two hundred years later, the situation repeated itself when the army was in decline and its budget slashed after the disintegration of the Soviet Union. People of means, education, intelligence, and ambition easily avoided the draft, leaving the ranks to be filled by the poor, the uneducated, the unhealthy, and the criminal element. In 2008, more than 80 percent of draftees came from blue-collar worker or peasant families. Almost 40 percent had been raised in orphanages or by single parents. More than 10 percent had criminal records or histories of alcohol abuse. General Sergei Shevchenko, deputy commander for education in the Russian Air Force, lamented that only a quarter of air force conscripts could be entrusted with weapons. In 2010, just as in 1710, a significant portion of soldiers were unmotivated, unhealthy, uneducated, and increasingly criminals.

Estate managers escorted the chosen serfs to the induction center often taking extra candidates in case the army rejected any of those selected by the village. In 1850, for example, the army accepted only 66,544 out of 139,002 men delivered for conscription. The army rejected men for being too short, too old, physically disabled, or diseased. There were persistent problems with peasants fleeing conscription, both before and after lots were drawn, and on the way from the village to collection points. In 1845, a law was passed making families responsible for runaway recruits. In his place, the family had to supply two recruits; if they could not do so, the head of the household was flogged or fined and could be exiled to Siberia. Because of this, villagers kept recruits under guard until they were delivered to the army.[7]

Once universal male service obligation became law in 1874, military commissions chose who would serve, relieving villagers and townspeople of the burden. In the spirit of maintaining the economic viability of families and villages, the new conscription law included exemptions based on family size, the number of able-bodied workers, and parenthood greatly reducing the size of the draft pool. When the time of service was reduced, the prospect of being drafted was far less terrifying for families, though still highly undesirable, and many did what they could to avoid it—legally and otherwise. The various constitutions of the Soviet period obligated all adult males to serve in the armed forces if called on. With the collectivization and mechanization of agriculture and the urbanization of society, military service, reduced to only two years, became viewed as inconvenient and personally onerous, but no longer potentially catastrophic to the family. Still, those with the wherewithal and imagination did what they could to avoid being taken. In the twenty-first century, though service is for only one year and exemptions are numerous, service remains unpopular and many avoid the draft.

After emancipation, parents, wives, and children often accompanied their menfolk to the district assembly point to say goodbye. Doleful scenes of parting were the norm, because soldiers were deliberately posted far from home to discourage desertion, and they would not be allowed leave during their six years. In the Putin era, the send-off of new recruits for their twelve months remains a somber affair. Scenes of recruits preparing to board trains in Omsk in 2022 are identical to the description given by a Siberian conscript in 1912, who noted sad distressed faces and tears in the eyes of family members (Figure 2.1).[8]

In the imperial period, there were limits to how many men the people would tolerate the government taking. There was an unstated threshold of the number of men the peasants thought they could lose and a point beyond which taking more was considered unfair and economically unviable. Landowners too felt there was a threshold that the regime should not cross. The government was keenly aware of the potential for resistance if it crossed that line—one of the few things that constrained its actions. This was one reason Alexander I resorted to calling up the *opolchenie* (temporarily serving volunteers from the free classes and serfs "loaned" to the army) in 1812 and Nicholas I in 1854.[9] The government felt constrained in its recruitment during the Polish insurrection of 1863 because it feared the peasantry would not submit to extraordinary conscription for what they considered a domestic affair. The Bolsheviks, less sensitive to popular feelings, provoked a major peasant revolt in Tambov province during the civil

Figure 2.1 New conscripts entraining to report for duty. iStock photos.

war because people perceived that too many men already had been taken even as the Red Army tried to take more.

Service Avoidance

Russians have engaged in a variety of behaviors, both legal and illegal, to avoid service, indicating that they do not consider themselves to be the property of the state and reject giving it their unquestioning obedience. Up to 1874, one way to avoid conscription was to hire a substitute. Estimates indicate that annually about 10,000 men agreed to serve as substitutes for a fee. Obviously, wealthy peasants were most able to take advantage of this opportunity. For example, between 1812 and 1857, the wealthier serfs on an estate owned by the Gagarin family spent roughly 34,000 rubles to purchase substitutes. Buying substitutes was so common that professional middlemen existed to facilitate their purchase. Those men willing to become substitutes were often state peasants, the urban poor, runaway serfs, or deserters who intended to take the money and then desert again. Landowners encouraged their serfs to buy substitutes from outside the estate to avoid the loss of labor. Substitutes were often sons rebelling against parental authority or the bonds of the village community, as well as men hoping to avoid judicial punishment.[10]

Besides substitutes, families could, in advance, purchase an exemption called a *rekrutskaia kvitantsiia* to save their son from conscription. In 1839, the army set 570 rubles as its price for an exemption. Because exemptions were transferable, a flourishing market developed. If a family had purchased a *kvitantsiia* and their son did not get taken, they could then sell it, often for a profit. In 1851, the usual price on the resale market was 1,000 rubles. Sometimes, serf owners sent more men to the army than requested because they had men they wanted to be rid of for a variety of reasons. In such cases, the army provided a receipt of credit toward the next round of conscription. When that time came, rather than present their receipts to the army, owners sold them to their serfs. In 1816, Prince Lieven recorded in his estate's ledger that he sold thirty-one exemptions: nine men paid the exorbitant sum of 2,000 rubles, eighteen paid 1,000, three paid 500, and one 250 rubles. How much of that money he passed on to the army he did not record.[11] The sale of exemptions and credits ended with the service reform of 1874, but until then, exemptions were another way in which the wealthy were better positioned to avoid conscription and leave the burden to fall on the poor.

Since the seventeenth century, men who desperately want to avoid service but cannot find a legal way out have resorted to a variety of illegal means to avoid being conscripted. These means include bribery, self-mutilation, and faking illnesses. Because the reputation of military service is so bad, even after the terms of service were reduced to just one year, men still to try to avoid service illegally. In the late nineteenth century, when families and villages were no longer responsible for supplying recruits, men simply failed to appear before the military commission when summoned. Some changed their name and moved to another town, hoping they would not be tracked down. Some cleverly got themselves arrested for petty crimes so they would be passed over for recruitment while in prison.

Social History of the Russians and Their Army

Under serfdom, peasants paid bribes to the village authorities, the bailiff or steward, or the serf owner to exempt their sons from the lottery or to place their family at the back of the "line." Serf owners would sometimes bribe doctors on military commissions to accept underage or unfit men so they could keep the strong and healthy working on the estate.[12] After 1874, bribing police chiefs, marshals of the nobility or one of the doctors on the military commission to declare one's son unfit became endemic. In many cases, a conscript or his parents made subtle offers of a bribe. Doctors sometimes slyly signaled that they would accept bribes, and some officials unabashedly solicited bribes. Doctors seem to have been very flexible in their pricing. In the 1870s and 1880s, some would accept as little as fifty rubles, while others demanded up to 800. In the case of peasants, it was the parents who usually came up with the money, but in the urban areas, young men typically paid bribes themselves.

Bribery of doctors continued into the Soviet period and to the present. Even though being taken into the Red Army did not mean financial ruin for one's family, some parents still thought it was worth paying to have their sons exempted from duty. During the Cold War, parents continued to pay doctors to keep their sons out of the army, especially during the Soviet-Afghan War (1979–89). In the 1980s, it was common knowledge in Moscow that the going rate for a medical exemption was between 1,000 and 2,000 rubles. The practice of bribing doctors was so common in the 2000s that some lawyers made being a go-between their specialty, charging clients the equivalent of $10,000.[13] The 2022 invasion of Ukraine led to an uptick in cases of bribery of doctors and members of military commissions to secure exemptions.

Self-injury by mutilation or poisoning, and faking illness have been common practices for hundreds of years. In the era of muzzle-loading muskets and rifles, men, with the connivance of their families, most often chopped off their trigger fingers or pulled their two front teeth (necessary to bite open paper cartridges). A drastic self-injury was to blind oneself in one eye. Self-mutilation was so prevalent that in 1766, Catherine II passed legislation setting punishment for it at twenty-five to fifty lashes and assignment to service anyway. If their injuries rendered them truly unfit, they were exiled to Siberia or assigned to a convict company.[14] Faking illnesses or poisoning oneself to create symptoms of bronchitis, tuberculosis, stomach ulcers, catarrh of the intestines, anemia, nephritis, cystitis, urethritis, diabetes, jaundice, and heart disease were common. With the advent of metallic cartridges, men resorted to pulling out more teeth (ten teeth missing from one jaw or fourteen teeth total was grounds for medical exemption) or giving themselves gum disease. Some would deliberately contract a combination of illnesses and injuries. Another inventive manipulation of the health requirements was to hire genuinely ill or injured men who were sure to be rejected to impersonate the conscript at induction points.[15]

With the growth of the Red Army to nearly five million men in the spring of 1941, a level of manning that remained that high for the rest of the Soviet period, military service became a normal, though undesired, experience for Soviet youth. Still, until the mid-1980s, compliance proved to be high and self-injury to avoid service rare. Gorbachev's policy of *glasnost* in the 1980s, for the first time gave opponents of conscription the ability to voice anti-military views on the radio, television, and in print, which encouraged youth to reject the inevitability of serving. The wars in Chechnya drove thousands of men to seek a wide range of deferments or to take their chances on getting arrested for draft evasion. In September 2022, during the war with Ukraine, the declaration of mobilization sparked an interest on how to injure oneself. In the week of the announcement, Google searches related to self-injury—using the phrase "*kak slomat' v domashniky usloviiakh*," meaning "how to break a hand at home"—showed a massive jump. Data for the search term went from too small to calculate to a fifty on Google's 100-point scale.[16]

Youths seeking to advance their careers through higher education considered military service a major nuisance. From the 1950s to 1967, university students had to interrupt their studies to serve their stint in the army. Between 1967 and 1982, the Ministry of Defense granted deferments that, for all intents and purposes, became exemptions that unfairly benefited the reasonably well-off, educated, white-collar urban population at the expense of the under-educated, poorly paid blue-collar and rural populations. The Ministry of Defense came to recognize that many young men entered higher education simply to avoid army service. One young man who had flunked out of a polytechnic institute in 1978 and was thereupon immediately drafted, protested by detonating a homemade bomb at his local military commission.[17] Much to the dismay of students, faculty, and parents, the Ministry of Defense eliminated deferments in 1982. Intense public criticism from academia and the educated urban population grew to the point that Gorbachev reinstated deferments in 1989.

Open resistance to the draft emerged in the 1980s. National minorities began to actively evade the draft as expressions of anti-Russian nationalism. In 1991, the last year of conscription in the Soviet period, 353,000 men refused to report for conscription and 2,500 deserted.[18] In the immediate aftermath of the Soviet Union's demise, groups sprang up in Moscow and Leningrad offering legal advice to help soldiers "work the system" to avoid being drafted. By 2001, 88 percent of draft-eligible men secured deferments annually, choosing between twenty-five different deferments. Putin's government considered abolishing deferments for higher education in 2004, but public backlash convinced them to back down.[19] In the first decades of the 2000s, anti-draft groups, now well-organized, graduated to using websites promising to help draft-aged men from all parts of Russia avoid service.

Military service continues to be unpopular. In 1997, 98,000 men evaded the draft. In 2001, 13 percent of men called up, especially those from the urban areas, opted not to report for duty. Since 2001, usually fewer than 5 percent of Muscovites eligible for the draft end up serving. In 2003, imitating late-nineteenth century behavior, 40,000 men simply ignored their draft notice and 50,000 secured exemptions. Two hundred thousand men avoided being called up in 2010 just because the army could not find them.

Volunteers

Despite decades of talk and legislative activity to transition the Russian Army to a professional contract army, conscription remains the primary form of peacetime recruitment. In the 2000s, when successive governments pushed for a volunteer army serving three-year contracts, the Ministry of Defense set the goal of manning half its force with volunteers. As of 2022, the armed forces claim to have surpassed that mark, reaching 70 percent of the men on three-year contracts. The generals of the high command hope to recruit better quality soldiers on contracts but still resist the complete ending of conscription. They insist on maintaining the army's right to take young men from society to sustain the idea that Russian men owe the state service, whether they like it or not. They also make money taking bribes to issue deferments. Overwhelmingly, however, *kontraktniki* begin their service as conscripts who are then coerced into taking contracts.[20]

Despite the army's poor reputation, a steady, if small, number of volunteers have found their way into service for the entirety of Russian history. Under serfdom, volunteers from a village or town could also be used to count against a village's or town's quota and often families, upon hearing that a man intended to volunteer, would pay them to substitute for their son. Before emancipation, volunteers (but not substitutes) were paid an enlistment bonus, most of which the army invested for them and paid back to them with interest upon discharge. Ordinary serfs could not volunteer without the landowners' consent; therefore, most volunteers came from free townsmen. During peacetime, in the Imperial Russian Army from 1874 to 1914 and in the Red Army from 1918 to 1991, the annual number of volunteers was insignificant. In the Putin era, contract service paid decent wages and succeeded in attracting volunteers (Figure 2.2). Most of them saw contract service as a way out of rural poverty—not as a way of expressing patriotism.

The contemporary Russian army leadership, mired in traditional thinking, was unprepared and unwilling to embrace the volunteer army concept until finally forced to in 2010. Then, never having had to reach out to young men to persuade them to volunteer, the Ministry of Defense had to establish a recruiting administration from scratch. Officers and men had to be assigned to recruiting duty and appropriately trained; slogans and advertising had to be developed; and infrastructure built. Since the 2010s, advertisements on television

Figure 2.2 Volunteers for the front, 1917. Wallach Division Picture Collection, The New York Public Library.

and billboards emphasize three themes: patriotism ("be a defender of the fatherland"), masculinity (being a soldier is the "manliest" occupation), and good pay. These themes failed to persuade the urban-educated younger generation to volunteer. Bright youths with promising futures mostly view a desire or willingness to serve in the rank and file as aberrant behavior. It is mainly the rural poor who volunteer for contract service for the pay.

When the war in Ukraine created the need for drastically more men to replace casualties, the army was forced to rely on voluntary recruitment because of the popular backlash generated by the partial mobilization in 2023. To increase the numbers of volunteers, the army, in 2023, intensified its messaging on the above themes, of which, a raise in monthly salary from the equivalent of $600 to $2,000 proved to be the most effective. Even with the high salary, the army still fell far short of its recruitment goal of 400,000 *kontraktniki*. Mid-way through the year, only about 40,000–50,000 men had volunteered.[21]

It also resorted to recruiting men out of prison or awaiting trial with promises of expunging their records, and thereby brought into the army tens of thousands of the "most villainous and mutinous" people, much like those who had plagued the army in the eighteenth century.

Soldatki

The effect of their menfolk's military service on wives and families varied in intensity from the imperial period to the modern era. During the era of serfdom, when a married serf was conscripted, his wife became a *soldatka* (plural *soldatki*) and like her husband was no longer a serf, so her place in a village on the estate of a landowner was no longer assured. It was permissible for a *soldatka* to accompany her husband to the army, but few couples chose this option; in the 1780s only 5 percent of wives accompanied their husbands, though about half of all soldiers were married.[22]

Most often, those soldiers who did have their wives with them were stationed in permanent garrisons or fortresses. If there was sufficient space, wives could live with their husbands in the barracks, but few regiments outside of St. Petersburg, Moscow, and Warsaw had barracks. Where there was no space for married couples, regiment commanders were supposed to provide funds for them to rent their own. Catherine II required that the army make reasonable attempts to employ those *soldatki* who accompanied their soldier husbands. Often, regiments hired wives to make tents, tailor uniforms, wash and mend clothes, or work in army hospitals. Male children born to soldiers became the property of the state and were expected to become soldiers themselves at the age of maturity. Daughters often married soldiers of their fathers' regiment.[23]

Soldatki of state-owned peasants who stayed behind were entitled to land and public assistance. It was not guaranteed a wife would get it, because for a woman to make use of land, she needed a working-age son. *Soldatki* on privately owned estates were in a more precarious situation. Although about 80 percent of women did stay in their home villages they were often mistreated and marginalized by their in-laws. If her own or her husband's family would not take her and any children in, then she often had no choice but to leave the village and make a life elsewhere. It was not unusual for *soldatki* who had no skills or capital to start a new life to fall into poverty and engage in criminal or dissolute behavior to survive.[24] Besides prostitution, the approximately 15 percent of *soldatki* who left their villages often engaged in trafficking unwanted infants between the countryside and foundling homes of Moscow and St. Petersburg. By law, *soldatki* were forbidden to remarry. Despite this prohibition, many *soldatki* who left their villages entered into illegal marriages by lying to or bribing priests, or by misrepresenting themselves as legally married. If such marriages were discovered, they were usually officially dissolved, the parties punished, and any children they produced were declared to be bastards. Others just cohabited with a man for economic and physical security while they waited for their husbands to finish their service. If a soldier returned home to find that his wife had remarried or borne children by another man, she could expect to be beaten unmercifully or even murdered with the tacit approval of the village.[25]

The prospect of conscription was terribly stressful for married serfs (wives were known to pray daily that their husbands would not be taken); the relief emancipation and the reduction of terms of service to six years brought must have been tremendous. No longer did the soldier or his wife lose their place in their community, and families were no longer permanently torn apart. Soldiers and *soldatki* maintained their right to land in the village. The army no longer allowed wives to accompany their husbands. If her husband was the head of the household, a *soldatka* could act in his stead. Still, six years of separation was a dismaying prospect and mistreatment at the hands of in-laws was not uncommon.

The 1874 law on universal military obligation exempted soldiers from the poll tax and stands as the first example of the government acknowledging that men who performed military service deserved some benefits. Beginning in 1912, the Russian government started paying *soldatki* a stipend (*paika*), further acknowledging that the state owed the families something for giving up their men and that the government had a responsibility to keep soldiers' families from being economically disadvantaged. It is notable that the initiative to establish the *paika* came from the State Duma and was not a gift of the sovereign. It was the elected representatives of the people who acknowledged that the state owed families some compensation for intruding into their lives and economic wellbeing.

During the First World War, Russia mobilized about sixteen million men, creating an unprecedented number of *soldatki*. Because of their large numbers and the common economic hardships caused by the war (especially inflation and goods shortages), peasant *soldatki* became, according to historian Mark Baker, "perhaps, [Russia's] first active, mass social movement of women."[26] Unified by the *paika*, soldiers' wives came to see themselves as having an identity separate from other wives; an identity reinforced by the envy of other married women in the village who considered the *soldatki* to be privileged. From the start of the war, in villages and small towns, *soldatki* began to act collectively in their interests. At their husbands' direction, they sought to prevent privatization of land that they considered detrimental to the village, even to the point of physical violence against government personnel. *Soldatki* banded together to demand increases in the *paika* due to the dire poverty to which many had been reduced because of their husbands' absence. They demonstrated and even rioted to protest the inflationary prices that made their lives miserable. *Soldatki* argued that because the government had taken away their breadwinners, it owed them and their families a living wage, this was perhaps the first popular articulation that the people considered the state to be responsible to the people and owed society for requiring men to do military service. In some villages, the *soldatki* went so far as to refuse to pay taxes until either the government raised the *paika* or sent their men home. Their shared poverty and suffering turned the *soldatki* into a significant political force. During the February Revolution in 1917, they marched in Petrograd with banners demanding the government raise the *paika*. In the months before October, they tended to support the Bolsheviks because they were the only party that promised peace, which meant the return of their husbands and financial recovery.[27]

In the aftermath of the Russian Civil War, *soldatki* disappeared as a social group because of the vastly diminished size of the Red Army, the end of the *paika*, collectivization of agriculture, rapid industrialization and accompanying urbanization, and the rising average marriage age. With the draft age set at 19, few men were married, so there was no critical mass of women to identify as soldiers' wives. During the Second World War, the Soviet government reinstated a type of *paika* in the form of payments to soldiers' families, if he had contributed to the family income regardless of his status in the household. The amount allotted was based on family size. The Soviet state treated the payments as necessary under the extraordinary circumstances of the war and not as an acknowledgement of a debt owed for the men doing their duty. The state discontinued the stipends at war's end.[28]

The Identification of soldiers' wives as an interest group revived in 2022 with the invasion of Ukraine. By this time, most soldiers were on contract and in their mid-twenties or older, and many were married. The mobilization of reservists in the autumn of 2022 galvanized wives to organize with the main goal of having their husbands released from service.

The Public's Image of the Army as an Institution and Symbol

How the Russian public viewed the army affected men's willingness to serve. Perceptions varied depending on class, nationality, race, religion, gender, and ideology. The peasantry, as noted above, generally had a negative view of the army because of the economic consequences. The land-owning nobility, meanwhile, had a mixed view of the army. On the one hand, before emancipation, the army deprived them of valuable labor. On the other hand, landlords and local officials appreciated that they could call in the army to enforce their power over the serfs. What's more, the army offered nobles employment and social status as officers. They willingly sent their sons to serve as officers, but after the military service reforms, they were not inclined to send their sons to serve as enlisted men.

With the gradual growth of the market economy and industry after emancipation, a sizeable portion of the economic and noble elite, as well as the nascent middle class and professionals, adopted a liberal political outlook. Part of this outlook included a jaundiced view of the military as a lever of tsarist power and its economic burden on the country. Liberal newspapers did not shy away from reporting unflattering incidents involving the military. Liberal-minded citizens typically avoided military service but supported the soldiers in wartime by donating money to soldiers' families and by serving in nongovernmental organizations such as the Red Cross and food kitchens to help soldiers' families. They established hospitals, funded medical trains, and opened their homes to convalescent soldiers. For them, supporting the soldiers did not equate to validating the army or the regime but was strictly a humanitarian gesture. During the Soviet period, the Communist Party elite gave lip service to the glory of the army but used their influence to keep their unwilling sons out of the military. After the Soviet period, the emergent wealthy elite of Russia has followed the Soviet pattern of using their social, and now also economic power to help their sons avoid service, while praising the army as emblematic of Russian nationalism.

National, ethnic, and religious minorities had additional reasons to be averse to military service. Jews had a strong aversion to service due to the exceptionally harsh treatment they received at the hands of anti-Semitic soldiers and officers. Muslims, other than Tatars, were exempt from service until 1916. The end of that exemption led to a revolt that was put down by regular army forces in what amounted to a near civil war. Under Soviet rule, not until the Second World War did the Red Army draft Central Asians. Then, they, like the Jews, suffered discrimination, brutality, and a glass ceiling to promotion. Poles and members of the Baltic States were also reluctant to serve, because they saw the imperial army as an alien occupying force to which they owed no loyalty or obligation. When then Baltic States, having gained their independence in 1921, were reabsorbed into the Soviet Union in 1940, made possible by the Nazi-Soviet Non-aggression Pact, the men again became subject to conscription. As before, Balts were held suspect and discriminated against for the rest of the Soviet period, which did not foster respect or affection for the Soviet state or military service. With societal approval, they began to evade the draft for nationalist motives in the mid-1980s.

Social History of the Russians and Their Army

Ukrainians, condescended to by Russians as their "little brothers," also harbored resentment of Russia. Nationalism emerged in the late nineteenth century and came into the open during the First World War. After the February Revolution, Ukraine sought autonomy first and then independence. The Bolsheviks reconquered it in 1918 and then had to overcome resurgent nationalism in 1944, which was not finally repressed for a decade—a situation duplicated in the Baltic states. The people of the Caucasus resisted Russian conquest for decades in the nineteenth century before being overcome. They unsuccessfully fought for independence during the civil war. Armenians, Georgians, and Azeris made failed bids for independence in the 1920s and 1930s. Their nationalist hopes resurfaced in the late 1980s. The Chechen wars of the 1990s and first decade of the 2000s continue the legacy of Great Russian imperialism that breeds resentment. All these peoples, then, had a strong aversion to serving in the Russian-dominated military.

Soldiers and Civilians

Besides taking men from families, the military created a negative impression by quartering the bulk of its men on the general population. Not until the 1880s did the army begin the transition to creating fixed garrisons with barracks and amenities for soldiers. It only completed the transition on the eve of the Russo-Japanese War; until then, peasants dreaded the prospect of soldiers being quartered with them. Soldiers caused peasant huts to be overcrowded, and their horses crowded the stables. Soldiers stole belongings, eggs, chickens, and pigs. They abused women, broke possessions, and disrupted peasant family life. Soldiers also fought peasants in the streets and occasionally murdered them. Maintaining an army unit in a village could be financially burdensome if officers requisitioned food and fodder, and then underpaid or failed to pay at all. In times when food was scarce, tensions rose between soldiers and their hosts and sometimes led to violence. Drunkenness, too, caused problems. Knowing the burden this imposed, the tsarist authorities sometimes quartered regiments in the villages of a district to punish disobedient peasants.

To Serve or Not to Serve

Because the army was used to conquer native peoples and then occupy and repress them in the name of Greater Russia or Soviet unity, it created a legacy of distrust and resentment among non-Russians. Some of the larger and most noteworthy rebellions against Moscow were the Pugachev Rebellion of 1773-75 and the Revolution of 1905. All of these, and thousands of other local protests, were violently put down by the army. The army's mission of maintaining domestic order and political domination of the central government meant repressing Russians, too. At the turn of the twentieth century, the army had fifty local battalions whose sole purpose was to enforce domestic order. From major and minor peasant and Cossack revolts in the eighteenth century, to workers' revolts in the early twentieth century, and nationalist revolts in the 1980s and 1990s, the appearance of the army on the scene spelt doom and misery to those the army came to suppress.

In contrast to peacetime, wartime generally brought society together in support of soldiers and the army. In the imperial and Soviet periods, the bulk of the population kept their love for their sons and brothers separate from their loathing or distrust of the state and army. During the recent war with Ukraine, however, a deeply divided Russian society exhibits both positive and negative opinions of the army. Pro-war Russians support the army and the soldiers, even if they are critical of its poor performance. Anti-war Russians feel sorry for the soldiers and hold the army high command and the military in low regard.

During the imperial period, the wealthy and poor alike donated money to help ease the plight of sick and wounded soldiers. From the mid-nineteenth century onward, during the last four wars of the tsarist era (the Crimean War, the Russo-Turkish War (1877-78), the Russo-Japanese War, and the First World War), peasants and urbanites wrote letters of support to soldiers at the front and sent them practical and fun gifts for Christmas, such as scarves, mittens, canned fruits, tea, and tobacco. At Easter, civic organizations would send the soldiers traditional Easter cakes. Members of the royal family and many cities adopted regiments and sent the soldiers gifts on holidays. During the Russo-Turkish War, peasants, workers, and the elites donated hundreds of thousands of rubles for the care of soldiers; during the Russo-Japanese War, millions; and during the First World War tens of millions. After the civil war, the government sponsored lotteries to raise funds for invalided veterans. During the Second World War, the authorities orchestrated multiple drives among civilians that succeeded in filling hundreds of boxcars with gifts for soldiers at the front. In addition, the Russian Orthodox Church encouraged people to donate two billion rubles to aid the wounded and for war-related charities. Communist Party and local government organizations followed the tsarist example of sponsoring letter-writing campaigns to boost soldiers' morale. However, popular support of soldiers had its limits. When the Communist Party asked people to donate their irreplaceable warm clothes to the army in the winters of 1941–42, and again the next year, the reaction was decidedly negative. Both warm clothes drives failed miserably.[29]

The war in Ukraine generated official calls for contributions to help the soldiers. In June 2022, Russian state media and officials began to advertise that the army needed help from the population. In response, the pro-Kremlin All-Russian People's Front launched a fundraiser for the needs of the army, focusing first on the ultra-wealthy who owed their success to Putin. The project was called "Everything for Victory," a reference to a Second World War slogan. Propagandist Vladimir Solovyov asked Russians to chip in for quadrocopter drones; the pro-Kremlin singer Denis Maidanov collected money for hats, belts, helmets, thermal imagers, and other equipment. Others solicited donations for laptop computers, sleeping bags, and first aid kits. The Ministry of Defense announced the creation of a fund to provide financial aid to military personnel. Women from throughout Russia, but mostly from the regions bordering Ukraine, baked cookies for the soldiers and collected millions of rubles for medical supplies, food, and expensive military equipment.[30] Organizers of these fundraising activities, however, complained of a general indifference among the population, so efforts to support the soldiers with gifts and morale-boosting letters shifted to the public schools where students were required to participate.

Supervised by their teachers, children sewed camouflage nets, stretchers, and sweatshirts, made trench candles, wrote letters to the men at the front and baked them Easter cakes. Thousands of school children made good-luck talismans for the soldiers with prayer-amulets sewn inside. In 2023, school children sent more than 50,000 stuffed animals to men at the front. Some schools had their students make key rings with charms, bags with wishes and prayers, and mittens. In April 2023, the focus was on sending Easter cards and in June "victory" letters. Throughout the school year, schools raised money to buy soldiers hygiene products, food, and military equipment.[31]

Over the centuries, society's attitude about abuses against civilians perpetrated by soldiers have undermined wartime support for the soldiery. Deserters and draft evaders during wartime were seen as shirking their duty and unfairly putting a greater burden on the soldiers who loyally manned the front lines. Deserters were known to be dangerous people. As fugitives from military justice, they often hid out in the woods or large cities and supported themselves by commiting crime. If they dared go home, neighbors whose sons were at the front were apt to turn them in. From Peter I's Great Northern War (1700–21) to Putin's war in Ukraine, deserters have been prone to use violence to avoid being apprehended.[32]

Deserters were not alone in causing problems for the civilian population. Russian soldiers have been as dangerous to their own populations as to those of the enemy. Tsarist soldiers victimized the peasants nearly as much as the French in the winter of 1812, robbing and raping peasants. Soldiers perpetrated atrocities against civilians during the First World War, the Russian Civil War, the war with Poland, and the conflicts with the Baltic States. In the civil war, soldiers carried out pogroms. Soldiers in retreat pillaged and raped as they fled the enemy. Both the Red and counter-revolutionary White armies committed atrocities against civilians suspected of supporting the other side. The Red Army, when not fighting the Whites, busied itself repressing anarchic peasant revolts and workers' protests, leaving a very bad taste in the mouths of those supposedly being liberated from oppression. The Red Army created ill will among the peasantry in 1941; while retreating in the face of the German onslaught, soldiers conducted a scorched earth campaign on Stalin's orders, burning villages and crops, and killing livestock. The return of the Red Army during the liberation of western Russia, Belorussia, and Ukraine in 1943 and 1944, was not all smiles and grateful hugs. Red Army soldiers raped multitudes of Soviet women and stole food from peasants who often did not have enough for themselves. Memories of these atrocities persisted for generations to contest the state's heroic imagery of the Red Army soldier.

During the Soviet-Afghan War, though the Soviet press praised the soldiers for performing their internationalist duty, the Soviet people had mixed emotions about the war and their sons' and brothers' role in it. Once it became known that Soviet soldiers routinely perpetrated atrocities against Afghan civilians, people began to look at soldiers negatively, and not just those who had served in the war. Drug-addicted soldiers returning from the war and violent crimes committed by veterans with PTSD further tarnished the military's image. Violent crimes, especially rape and murder, by soldiers returning from the war in Ukraine are regularly reported in the press, counteracting Putin's efforts to hold up soldiers as ideal citizens. A vague sense of unease about the potential for criminal violence among soldiers returned from the front began to pervade Russian society in 2022. In 2023, veterans of the mercenary Wagner Group averaged a murder every other day. Veterans of the regular army have gained a reputation for rape and murder on nearly the same scale. Publicly lauded as heroes, in private many Russians view soldiers as potentially violent criminals.[33]

Popular anti-militarism became manifest in the Gorbachev era, fed by the ambiguous nature of the Soviet-Afghan War, the publicity given to hazing, and fear of nuclear war. The military's reputation suffered greatly with the Mathias Rust affair in which a young German man flew a small private aircraft across the USSR and landed in Red Square, successfully evading hundreds of billions of rubles worth of air defenses. The Soviet people concluded that expenditures on the military were wasted and contributed to their low standard of living. Finally, the use of the army to suppress domestic opposition among independence-seeking nationalities in 1989 and 1990, and their role in the August Coup against Gorbachev in 1991, nearly destroyed what was left of the positive image of the Soviet military.

To Serve or Not to Serve

Putin, intending to make role models of soldiers, has undermined his cause by recruiting veterans to act as street thugs to intimidate liberal political opposition and to break up any forms of anti-Putin or anti-war public gatherings, much like Mussolini's Black Shirts and the Nazi's Brown Shirts in the 1920s and 1930s.[34] The words of Walter von Molo, who described the plight of those Germans who had not supported Hitler, are applicable to the social rift in twenty-first-century Russia between those who do and do not support Putin and his militarization of society.

> ... look at the grief-furrowed faces, look at the unutterable sadness in the eyes of the many who did not take part in the glorification of the shadowy side of our natures, who could not leave their homes, because we are talking here of many millions of people for whom there was no other place on earth other than their own land which was gradually transforming itself into a huge concentration camp, in which there would be only different grades of prisoners and warders.[35]

Putin increasingly has called on—even expects—soldiers and veterans to join the ranks of warders.

The popular image of the Russian army since the collapse of the Soviet Union is as mixed as always. In many ways, it evokes national pride, but not to the extent that significant numbers of Russian youth want to enlist or that parents favor sending their sons to it or paying higher taxes to improve it. The massacre of Ukrainian civilians in Bucha, Andriivka, Izium and elsewhere, and the inept conduct of the war against Ukraine, like the war in Afghanistan, has undermined public confidence in the army and degraded the willingness of wives and mothers to send their men to the army. In sum, the aversion to service and ambivalent views of veterans has remained strong for more than 300 years.

CHAPTER 3
THE OFFICER CORPS

The main themes of this chapter are the officer corps and its relationships with civil society and the soldiers in the context of its self-image and self-identity (its military culture) and how little its culture changed across the centuries despite radical changes in political and social systems; Putin's officers share most of the values, attitudes, and culture of Peter I's officers. Overall, from the tsarist period to the present, Russian military culture promotes an outlook in which officers view themselves as heroic defenders of Russia, worthy of admiration simply for wearing the uniform, even though, until the late nineteenth century, service was more of an avocation than vocation. Only in the late nineteenth century did officers begin to see themselves as a corps with a corporate identity and defined group interests that the Ministry of Defense and General Staff worked to defend.

For most of the imperial period, most officers saw themselves the way the tsars expected—as servitors of the sovereign rather than of the nation or the people. During the Soviet period, officers were encouraged to see themselves as servants of the Communist Party. This was mildly successful in the early years but weakened after the Second World War. In the twenty-first century, under the Russian Federation, Putin has turned the clock back and seeks to have the officers regard him as the object of their service. How successful this will be is yet to be seen.

No matter the political structure, the officer corps understands its interests and pursues them in such a way that indicates it believes it is the most important institution in Russia and that it represents what is best for Russia, meaning, what is good for the officer corps is good for Russia; in extreme cases some of the military leadership acts as though Russia exists to serve the army. In that vein, officers feel superior to civilians—sometimes even superior to the commander-in-chief—and try to guide the civilian government to serve its interests in the name of serving Russia. Culturally, officers see themselves as "real" Russian patriots deserving of respect and not accountable to civil society. They assign themselves a status superior to the rest of society. This attitude, this chapter argues, further deepens the rift between the army and society.

What the Officer Corps Wants from Society and What Society Expects of the Officer Corps

From the Russian army's origins to the present, officers have wanted high social status, respect, a positive image, and to be above criticism. They have expected the state to ensure these conditions. Society, meanwhile, has had mixed expectations of the officer corps. During the imperial period, the nobility wanted to keep service for officers as exclusive to their estate as possible, for military service to enable social advancement up the table of ranks, and to provide employment. Commoners had negative expectations of the officer corps, seeing officers as agents of autocracy and oppression. After Minister of Defense General Dmitri Miliutin's military reforms of the 1860s and 1870s opened the officer corps to non-nobles, some commoners began to see service in the officer corps as a means of social mobility. During the Soviet period, the Communist Party expected the officer corps to be subservient to it, and the people expected the Party to keep the officers in line. Contemporary Russians expect the officer corps to be professional and law-abiding.

In the tsarist era, officers had high social status among the nobility in contrast to the low popular opinion of them. In the initial years of the Soviet era, officers had low social status overall. The Soviet state held up workers and engineers as ideal citizens. That changed with the Second World War. In its aftermath, until the war in Afghanistan, the officer corps enjoyed high social status and a positive image. Anti-militarism surfaced during the Gorbachev era and carried into the post-Soviet era leading to a rapid decline in popular regard for the officer corps, from which it has not yet recovered. Since the mid-1980s, the public

The Officer Corps

has demanded that individual officers be held accountable to society for their misdeeds. Under autocracy, it was in the monarchy's interest to uphold the status and image of the officer corps, but since the Revolution, the Soviet and post-Soviet regimes have been less energetic in protecting the officer corps' image until the invasion of Ukraine.

Peter I can be considered the founder of what would become the Russian army officer corps. Although service as officers in his army was open to all classes of society and foreigners, Peter's main source of officers was the nobility, who, from 1714 on, began their service as enlisted soldiers in the Guards regiments (they were to guard the life of the tsar and the royal family). Officers who rose through these regiments became the social elite of Russian society for as long as the Romanov dynasty lasted. From the reign of Peter to 1736, nobles were a servitor class and were required to serve the sovereign either as officers or civil servants from age 16 for life.[1] The statutes abolishing these requirements were drawn up by Peter III in 1762 and implemented by his successor and widow Catherine II. Thereafter, nobles served on a voluntary basis, gaining commissions either by enrolling in regiments and serving an apprenticeship or graduating from one of the few cadet corps.

After service was no longer compulsory, it was rare for a noble family to not have at least one of its sons become an officer. The wealthier the family, the more likely that more than one son would serve. It was an exceptionally impoverished noble who served for the money, as pay was rather low until the late-nineteenth century. Few chose to make the army a career. Most served for only a few years in their youth and then returned to their family estates or went on to other endeavors. Officers could enter or leave active service as the mood struck; a practice begun under Peter I when most officers tended to their estates when not on campaign.[2]

Military Culture under the Old Regime

Across the ages, the army's officers have considered themselves socially and morally superior both to their soldiers and civilians. This attitude originated naturally from the division of society into noble and non-noble estates, with officers drawn from the noble estate having rights, privileges, and advantages denied to commoners. It was the norm for officers to flaunt their status.

The desire of the Russian nobility to maintain the high social status of the officer corps—mostly by denying access to commoners, even at the expense of national security—was strong all the way up until Alexander II's reforms. This is aptly demonstrated by the attitude of the Moscow noble society in 1855. In January of that year, Nicholas I, shortly before his death, gave instructions for citizens' militia units (*opolchenie*) to be formed to reinforce the regular army during the Crimean War. The nobles of Moscow Province convened an extraordinary meeting where they elected a retired general to form and lead a division of some 254 officers and 12,000 men. The assembly agreed that all officers had to be nobles elected by the hereditary nobility. Many commoners, aspiring to elevate their social status, presented themselves for selection but were rebuffed and directed to enlist as soldiers in the regular army. It was then suggested that commissions be granted to men of the personal nobility, earned through civil service. The assembly voted down this suggestion. In the end, the noble assembly ended up electing only 139 men fit for duty and sent the division off to war without enough leaders rather than share their status with commoners.[3]

After a decade of noble opposition, Alexander II promulgated the new Law on Universal Military Obligation of 1874, allowing nobles to be drafted as privates and for all social classes to apply to *junker* schools to earn commissions. Miliutin had wanted to open cadet corps to commoners as well but succumbed to pressure to keep them exclusively noble. While Miliutin consciously used the military as a vehicle for social change, that was not his primary motive. He was driven by the fact that the army needed more and better officers than the nobility would ever provide, and undoubtedly in his decades of service he had observed highly competent soldiers who would have made good officers.

As a result of these and other reforms, fifty years later, with over half of officers now coming from common social origins, officers mixed more readily with noble and non-noble civilians. Officers were accepted into civic groups that included a wide range of interests, such as bicycling, gardening, temperance, archeology, and aviation. The Esperanto Society and Society of Composers of St. Petersburg welcomed officers, as did the charitable organization *Bratskaia pomoshch* in Riga. The *Bogatyr* patriotic history club with branches in several cities was a mix of officers and civilians. Moscow's Merchant Society accepted officers into its membership, as did the exclusive St. Petersburg sailing club. Local and regional noble societies welcomed officers as members.[4] Local noble societies and municipal governments regularly sponsored social events for officers to celebrate major military anniversaries and regimental holidays. The growing interaction between officers and civilians challenged the myth, repeated by Guards officers, that the officer corps was a caste apart from civil society.

The prestige of officers, specifically Guards officers, was highest among Russian high society in St. Petersburg. Officers were invited to all the dances in the capital during the season. Nobles sought to marry their daughters to Guards officers, either to maintain or enhance their family's social status. Guards officers could only marry into the wealthy hereditary nobility. These men cared little about what most civilians—nobles and commoners alike—thought of them. According to the memoirs of Vladimir Trubetskoi, referring to the years immediately before the First World War, "In those days a military man, and especially a young cavalry man, as a rule would treat civilians with a certain disdain and sense of superiority."[5] When General N. A. Vintulov' celebrated his fiftieth anniversary of military service, the highest praise a newspaper gave him was that "he is popular in St. Petersburg society."[6] During the February 1917 Revolution, the arrogance of Guards officers made them most likely to be murdered by revolutionaries and soldiers. Officers of ordinary line units, typically being of modest means, tended to be less proud and more agreeable in the company of civilians and could marry women from any social category (Figure 3.1).

Evidence that opening the officer corps to non-nobles—not just soldiers up from the ranks—attracted many commoners is that by 1912, 52 percent of all officers were from non-noble social origins.

Social History of the Russians and Their Army

Figure 3.1 Bain News Service, publisher. Russian Army officers, *c.* 1910 (between and *c.* 1915). Photograph. https://www.loc.gov/item/2014690036/.

Commoners were more likely motivated to serve to take advantage of the social mobility that a commission provided rather than for patriotic reasons. Non-noble officers' families began traditions of serving, identifying their personal interests with those of the army.[7] On becoming an officer, a commoner automatically earned personal nobility, raising him above his common social origins. He could even earn hereditary nobility if he rose high enough in rank. Once they rose in society, such officers tended to distance themselves from their former social estate and identify with their new one. Officers from common social origins, while not overly attached to the tsarist autocratic system, lamented, like their hereditary noble fellow officers, the loss of social status with the fall of the monarchy in 1917.[8]

The tsars helped maintain the prestige and image of the army by forbidding criticism of officers in the press. In the late imperial period, Alexander III and Nicholas II encouraged officers to duel any civilian who cast aspersions on the army or an officer's honor. Furthermore, officers charged with crimes committed in civil society could be tried only by courts-martial.

The Persistence of Tsarist Military Culture

To a surprising extent, given the anti-military nature of Marxist ideology and the pre-Revolutionary Bolshevik Party, much of the tsarist military culture survived the Revolution and carried over into the new Red Army. The Bolshevik regime intended to transform Russia into a classless egalitarian society. The former noble and bourgeois elites became non-persons, losing their property, wealth, and social status. Many Bolsheviks wanted to replace the army with a citizens' militia, one without an officer corps with corporate interests. Those Bolsheviks who wanted a standing army prevailed in the political debates of the 1920s, but to make the army reflect society as much as possible and to reduce the social distance between officers and men, ranks were abolished, uniforms were unadorned, and officers were addressed as comrade.

During the 1920s and 1930s, neither society nor the Soviet media held officers in high regard. In fact, they would be distrusted by the people, the state, and the Party, which harbored fears of a "Bonapartist" military coup. The Communist Party was so distrustful of the officer corps that it created commissars who, during the civil war, shared command with the officers to ensure the latter's loyalty. To advance their careers, officers were expected to join the Communist Party, participate alongside civilian Party members in civic and economic activities, and occasionally serve in Soviet government at levels commensurate with their rank.[9]

The initial cohort of leaders of the new Red Army was a mix of officers of the old army, though they were distrusted but whose expertise was essential to organize the new army, revolutionaries who joined during the civil war and earned commissions for battlefield performance, and new officers recruited exclusively from the working and peasant classes. In the immediate aftermath of the civil war, the peacetime army suffered serious discipline issues that led the new

Bolshevik high command to seek more traditionally hierarchical officer-enlisted relations and to eliminate GlavPUR and its commissars, thus giving the officers sole command. An intense political struggle ensued between socialist ideologues and pragmatic military-oriented Party members. The result was that the commissars stayed, but the officers had sole command, and the military was constituted as a small standing force alongside a large territorial militia.[10] Perhaps because of the need for social distance to enhance their authority in the interest of discipline, and their undeniable status as the heroes who won the civil war and secured the Bolshevik seizure of power, and that they were now the guarantors of the revolution, Soviet "Red Commanders"—to the dismay of Bolshevik purists—quickly adopted the same expectations as their tsarist predecessors: an elevated social status and public image, and immunity from public criticism. These expectations, however, would be unmet for two decades.

In the mid-1930s, the high command managed to restore some of the trappings of the old army that enhanced the officer corps' image. Ranks were reintroduced in 1935, as was the privilege of being tried only in courts-martial. Dress uniforms were issued, and dance lessons became part of the curricula in the military schools. Censorship prevented any popular expression critical of the military. Despite these changes, because of officers' low social status, low pay, and a general popular aversion to military service, the Red Army had trouble recruiting officers.

Victory in the Second World War elevated the social status and image of the officer corps. From 1945 to the late 1980s, the army had no difficulty recruiting officers. Pay was raised, dress uniforms became more ornate, and officers of the high command normally participated in major public ceremonies. Officers adopted a socially superior attitude toward their men, probably because they had higher educations, were well paid, and the state and society held them in high esteem. In the 1960s and 1970s, service as an officer was always listed in the top ten most respected careers in polls taken of high school and college youth. Women saw officers as attractive mates, for their prestige as well as their stable incomes, guaranteed housing, and free medical care.[11]

Challenges to the Officer Corps' Image

The status of the officer corps began to fall as tensions between civilian society and the officers rose in the mid-1980s, when Mikhail Gorbachev became General Secretary of the Communist Party. Gorbachev and his reform policies caused a precipitous decline in popular regard for the officer corps. Gorbachev's goal was to end the Cold War, end the war in Afghanistan, and rein in military spending to halt the USSR's economic decline. The methods he used to reform the system inadvertently caused the officer corps to lose favor in the eyes of the people. Specifically, it was his program of *glasnost* that allowed people to express negative opinions about the officer corps and to hold individual officers accountable for misdeeds. Public criticism of the army and of officers by name had never been allowed in Russian history, so the officer corps was unprepared for it.

As noted in earlier chapters, *glasnost* led to the founding of the Union of Committees of Soldiers' Mothers (UCSM). This organization spearheaded the criticism of the army as an institution and, at first only obliquely, of the officer corps, particularly for hazing. Later, in the post-Soviet era, they targeted individual officers. The military high command did not have a unified response. Some generals denied there were problems. Others acknowledged the problems but placed the blame on society rather than the army. In general, an anti-military tone crept into Soviet society between 1988 and 1991, notably among the liberal intelligentsia, supported by Gorbachev's leadership team.[12]

Initially, the rise of anti-militarism was due to public knowledge of atrocities committed in the Soviet-Afghan War and the maltreatment of soldiers by officers in the combat zone. In the late 1980s, Gorbachev's political changes allowed for the election of a Congress of Peoples' Deputies and Republic legislatures. These, in short order, formed special committees and commissions to investigate corruption, malfeasance, and a host of abuses by senior officers. Soon, officers' misuse of funds and supplies, as well as the deaths of civilians involved in street demonstrations at the hands of soldiers, were widely publicized. The extent to which defense spending negatively affected the quality of life of civilians became known and caused widespread discontent. One man wrote to a popular weekly magazine in 1989 declaring: "But it's time to ask our Ministry of Defense … where they got those insatiable appetites, and why there was no serious attempt to control them. What kind of closed agency is the Army, and will it be held accountable to the people …?"[13] Popular respect for officers dropped. Recruiting new officers became a challenge; junior officers resigned from the service by the tens of thousands.

Things worsened when Gorbachev allowed military leaders to be publicly blamed and held accountable for the deaths of civilians at the hands of soldiers under their command. The first victim of this was General Igor Rodionov, who had been sent to break up nationalist demonstrations in Tbilisi, Georgia, in April 1989. During these demonstrations, soldiers killed nineteen civilians, and images of the mayhem were distributed in the Soviet media, causing an outcry among civilians. An investigation by the Congress of People's Deputies declared that "Generals K. A. Kochetov, I. N. Rodionov, and Iu. T. Efimov bear personal responsibility for these violations and oversights which led to the tragic consequences."[14] Another military intervention, in Baku in January 1990, during the fight between the Armenians and the Azeris, left well over 100 civilians dead, again blackening the image of the military leadership. When reservists were called up to participate in the intervention, the UCSM successfully rallied mothers to prevent the mobilization.[15]

Public support for the military and respect for the officer corps hit its lowest point during the Soviet period as a result of the August Coup of 1991, in which the Minister of Defense attempted to use the army against Gorbachev. Some high-level unit commanders supported the coup; some plotted to resist it. Most officers, however, refused to take sides not being sure who was really in charge (Gorbachev or Russian Federation President, Boris Yeltsin) and whose government was legitimate.[16] The cumulative effect was to sow popular mistrust of the officer corps.

Post-Soviet Challenges

The expectations of the Army of the Russian Federation's officer corps are the same as those of the former Soviet and the Imperial Russian

The Officer Corps

Army officer corps. The officers want to return to the high social status they enjoyed before Gorbachev's reforms. They also want the government to abolish the public's ability to criticize them or hold them liable for misconduct. Only the second of these expectations has been met. With the demise of socialism and the introduction of a market economy, Russian society became more stratified based on wealth. This put the officer corps at a disadvantage because, in the 1990s, pay was generally inadequate, and talented, hardworking, educated men could create better and more socially prominent lives for themselves as civilians. The end of the Cold War made military service seem less important than before.

Because of the drop in status and better opportunities elsewhere, more than 150,000 officers either left the army voluntarily or retired early. Dozens of military schools closed. Many officers who stayed felt little pride in their status. One officer said, "We serve in the army because we don't know how to do anything else. Who else would want to steal as an officer today if they could work in a bank?"[17] The only thing that kept the army from being undermanned in officers during the 1990s was the drastic reduction in the size of the military.

Following Gorbachev's precedent, President Yeltsin, continued to allow public scrutiny of the officer corps and encouraged that it be held accountable. Yeltsin went so far as to create a government office to handle civilian complaints against the military. The personnel of this administration made good-faith, if not very successful, efforts to bring corrupt and abusive officers to account.[18] It was widely accepted that not just the UCSMR, but all Russian civil society, had the right and obligation to monitor the behavior of the officer corps. Needless to say, most of the officer corps rejected this idea, resisted public scrutiny, and lost faith in Yeltsin as their commander-in-chief. Despite the officer corps' attempts to discredit the mothers' efforts, a survey conducted in November 2004 revealed that 72 percent of women believed that the efforts of the UCSMR benefitted Russia. Only 5 percent agreed with the army high command that their activity was detrimental to national defense.[19] Some unit commanders did work with the mothers in good faith and others tried to co-opt the mothers to marginalize perceptions that they were undermining commanders' authority.[20]

Social History of the Russians and Their Army

In an effort to improve the officer corps' position in Russian society, officers ran for public office at the local, regional, and national levels. A total of 162 officers secured places on ballots for the 1995 elections to the State Duma. The Ministry of Defense handpicked 119 of them. Only ten were elected, two from the Ministry of Defense's list of candidates and eight independents. Almost all the officers who did not get elected came in last in their races.[21] This was a far cry from the 11,900 officers who had served in Soviet government in 1989, nearly all of whom ran on the Communist Party ticket, which virtually guaranteed election. Officers fared no better in regional and local elections. Clearly, the officer corps was not seen as a trusted source of representatives by the civilian masses.

The situation repeated itself in 2024. Vladimir Putin encouraged veterans of the war in Ukraine to run for local office to become the new local elites. In fact, most men who filed for candidacy were rejected by the parties they hoped to represent. Local officials jealously guarded their political prerogatives and many simply did not want veterans of the war to serve alongside them in the municipal government. Only a mere handful of those that did make it onto the ballots succeeded in being elected.[22] Veterans did better, however, in the 2024 regional parliamentary elections—which many consider fraudulent—in which 308 of 423 veterans on the ballots gained seats making them 7.8 percent of the 3,910 candidates elected. All but six of them were members of Putin's United Russia party, which dominated the suspect elections overall.[23]

The officer corps supported the election of Vladimir Putin to the presidency in 2000 in large part because he promised to restore the military budget and increase pay, which would raise both their status and quality of life. Putin did follow through on the pay increases. What the officers wanted even more than higher pay was to end public scrutiny and criticism of their actions. Not until 2022, did Putin outlaw all criticism of Russia's military endeavors, past and present, under the term "discrediting the army," and shut down the numerous mothers' and wives' activist organizations, declaring them to be "foreign agents" or "undesirable" organizations. He took these measures not only to protect the officers, but also to prevent criticism of his war against Ukraine.

The Officer Corps

Despite these measures, Putin was unable to eliminate criticism of the officer corps, largely because the war with Ukraine created another challenge to its image and prestige due to the phenomenon of the pro-regime, pro-war "milblogger." Milbloggers include former army officers, men with ties to government officials, former security service officers, and journalists for state-run news outlets, who use various social media platforms on the internet to deliver live updates, critiques, and analysis of the course of the war, not only to inform their followers, but also to criticize the officer corps for failing, in their opinions, to properly conduct the war. These bloggers are Russian ultra-nationalists who regularly share in-depth information from the frontlines with their hundreds of thousands of followers. Because milbloggers are pro-war and support Putin's militant foreign policies, Putin has been hesitant to rein them in. They have ignored his numerous statements cautioning them. Finally, in 2023, Putin ordered the arrest of Igor Girkin, a.k.a. Igor Strelkov, for going too far in criticizing not only the incompetence of the generals leading the war, but also Putin for his failures as commander-in-chief. Although, since then, milbloggers still accuse generals by name and the high command of massive incompetence, they carefully exempt Putin from any responsibility. Their often harsh, insightful, knowledgeable, and informed criticisms casts serious doubts among the Russian public about the competence of the officer corps and the advisability of sending their men to the army.[24] Overall, the internet has proven to be a thorn in the side of the army because it enables civilians and soldiers to voice complaints and dissatisfaction with the military leadership.

Corruption and the Officer Corps' Image

Two main areas that have provoked public ire and generated activism against the officer corps are corruption and the physical and psychological abuse of soldiers. Corruption has been endemic to the officer corps from its origins. Seeing themselves as guardians of the Russian nation and culture, officers feel no shame in demanding the best of Russia's resources and as much of the national budget for the military as they can possibly get, without regard to its affects on civil society. As leaders of the armed forces who made personal sacrifices in their climb to the top, senior officers often feel that they are entitled to a superior standard of living which, because their pay does not allow for it, enables them to justify corruption in the form of embezzlement, bribery, and diversion of government property to attain a high quality of life, even if it were deleterious to military preparedness.[25] This thinking binds the military elites together in a negative relationship to their civilian counterparts and to civilian society in general.

The main area of corruption under the tsarist regime was officers manipulating allowances for food, uniforms, and fodder. The main actors in corrupt schemes were regiment commanders and officers in the intendancy. Regiment commanders would claim they needed more money than they actually did to feed and clothe the men and to feed the horses, or they would take the designated allotment and buy inferior products at a price lower than the amount they claimed was necessary and pocket the difference. This practice was so widespread as to become normative. The high command habitually turned a blind eye to it. As part of his reforms, Minister of Defense Miliutin, in the 1870s, to cut down on this malfeasance, took the purchase of forage out of the hands of regiment commanders and created five-man commissions with the division commander as their head to do the purchasing. When the British military attaché asked General Chernaiev what he thought of the change, Chernaiev cynically replied, "There will now be five robbers instead of one."[26] Indeed, Miliutin's efforts were for naught. A British military attaché observing the Russian army during the Russo-Japanese War wrote that several officers openly bragged about how much money they made by stealing from the funds allocated for the upkeep of their squadrons. Because these corrupt practices were not made public under the autocracy, they did little harm to the officer corps' image. During the years 1906-1914, however, when the Duma had oversight of military expenditures, officers were publicly held to account for malfeasance. The "Trial of the 66" in 1911, exposed the intendency of the Moscow military district for massive fraud in uniform procurement. Confirming the words of the British military attaché noted above, "My own firm belief is that robbery on a big scale is practiced by a very large proportion of those Russian officers who are entrusted with public money."[27]

During the Soviet era, corruption was largely confined to logistics officers and members of military commissariats. Because all supply matters were now handled by the logistics branch, commanders had few opportunities to cheat the government. Before the Second World War, the Red Army vigorously prosecuted corrupt officers. One of the more sensational crimes of misappropriating government property that was made public occurred in 1925. Twelve men of the administration of the port of Leningrad, including six army officers, were executed for selling more than 1,000 tons of government goods for more than two million rubles. Eighteen others were given prison terms ranging from six months to ten years.[28] A high-profile case of harshly punished corruption was that of Marshal Grigory Kulik, a civil war-era pal of Stalin's, whom Stalin had executed in 1952 for reportedly stealing millions of rubles worth of state property. Generals with powerful friends, however, could expect to be shielded from punishment. After the Cold War, and especially in the 1960s through the 1980s, senior officers—mostly colonels and generals—were occasionally prosecuted for misappropriating building materials and soldier labor to build themselves dachas, a practice that continued into the post-Soviet era.[29]

Corruption further damaged the public image of the officer corps and lowered civilian respect for officers beginning in the late 1980s. With *glasnost,* the anti-militarism of the emerging free press in the USSR increased year by year. Journalists sought to expose corruption to deliberately damage the reputation of the officer corps. In the 1990s and 2000s, the advent of investigative journalism and then social media brought the officer corps under the closest scrutiny it had ever seen. Corruption in the 1990s mostly involved officers selling military equipment and supplies. Like their Imperial Army forbears, some commanders hired their soldiers out to collective farms but kept the soldiers' pay for themselves. Many justified it because of their low wages, saying they needed to do so just to survive. In 1997, the Main

Military Procurator's Officer investigated twenty-one generals for corruption.[30]

Between 2011 and 2020, Putin followed through on his promises to fund the modernization of the army's armament, equipment, and facilities by pouring twenty trillion rubles ($300 billion) into research and development, production, and construction. This vast sum presented untold numbers of opportunities for corruption. In 2013, the Procurator General's Office estimated that there were more than 7,000 violations related to corruption, with the majority in the realm of defense procurement, that cost the armed forces 4.4 billion rubles. In the first half of 2013, more than 1,100 officers and civilian employees of the military were convicted of malfeasance-related offenses, and 505 people were subjected to criminal charges. Besides skimming off the top and taking bribes to steer contracts to favored companies, officers engaged in corrupt practices in the areas of military real estate, provisioning, the supply of heating and electricity to garrisons, and in schemes in which funds for unperformed construction work were pocketed. Between 2014 and 2017, the armed forces lost at least 212 billion rubles to corruption. In 2018, more than 2,800 officers and civilian administrators in league with them were convicted of financial crimes.[31] Media coverage of corruption by officers, especially high-ranking officers, degraded the status and respect of the officer corps, and demoralized honest officers.

Despite the negative image created by the scale of corruption, the military has not shied from reporting it in the media. The army publishes notices of the trials and their results in its daily newspaper *Krasnaia zvezda*. Yet, even with this apparent transparency, people suspect that the authorities look the other way at the corruption of Putin's insiders and cronies—as long as they are in his good graces. The 2024 "purge" of deputy defense ministers, after Minister of Defense Sergei Shoigu was replaced, all arrested on charges of corruption, convinced many that it was politics rather than corruption that had led to their demise. The fact that they had been suspected of corrupt practices for years, but were only arrested after their benefactor fell out of favor, seemed to confirm that some officers were allowed to steal based on in- and out-group associations.[32]

Officers' Treatment of Soldiers

Another area that has alienated the officer corps from society is its relationship with the soldiers. Chapter 1 examined the officer-enlisted relationship from the soldiers' perspective. Here we look at the relationship from the officers' perspective and how their treatment of soldiers affected society's perception of the officer corps. Across regime changes, officers' treatment of soldiers flowed directly from their views of what constituted a proper relationship between leader and led. In the imperial period, this relationship was grounded in Russia's social stratification, with nobility and wealth counting more than rank for the right to exercise power. After the Revolution, with social equality the norm, the relationship changed, with officers being acknowledged as superior to soldiers due to constituted authority. From the founding of the first cadet corps and all other military educational institutions to the present, instruction in the theory and practice of leadership in which the leader motivates the led to obey willingly rather than commanding using formal authority to compel obedience, has never been part of the curricula.[33] The officer corps, seemingly by nature, has always relied on fear-based compulsion.

During the imperial period, officers saw their relationship with the soldiers as paternal. A quote from American politician Albert J. Beveridge, who visited Russia in 1904, neatly sums up the historic attitude of officers to their men, which he noted was a reflection of patriarchal civilian society: "And in the military establishment, again the soldiers of the Czar are the children of the Czar; the soldiers … are the children of the general; the colonel is father of his regiment, the captain of his company. Thus, a paternal and filial relationship exists which you may see nowhere else on earth."[34] The idea that officers and men should see themselves in a paternal relationship was included in regulations as early as the 1764 Instructions to Colonels, which required them to "look after their subordinates as fathers look after their children"[35] The familial imagery was meant to mitigate the incredibly unfeeling, brutal, and uncaring treatment of soldiers by officers that had existed for at least a century. The idea was that if officers saw the men as their children, they would treat them better.[36] Society was largely ignorant of this abuse up to the emancipation. Those who were aware were largely indifferent to it, if for no other reason than civilians too suffered physical abuse at the hands of social superiors and government authorities.

Even though officers considered it beneath them to engage in conversations with soldiers, many officers truly believed that the soldiers saw them as father figures. Aleksei Ignat'ev remembered that he thought he was getting close to the men as a "father commander," but: "It was not till later that I realized that the human being they felt most intimate with was my semi-illiterate [sic] NCO assistant, Gavrilov, and that for them I was still 'the master,' just carrying on the almost obligatory traditions of our 'landlord' regiment regarding relations with the rank and file."[37] What most officers failed to comprehend was that officers, in the eyes of soldiers, were representatives of the tsarist state who represented the interests of the nobility and was thus an alien force hostile to the interests of peasants and working class soldiers. Just as officers were wont to see the soldiers as "gray masses," the different social origins of officers in the late imperial period meant nothing to the soldiers. Officers, commoners or nobles, were all the same to them.

With the emancipation of the serfs, society's attitude changed along with the soldiers'. After 1861, as the ideas of citizenship and individual self-worth spread, society began to question the paternal relationship, and the abuse that came with it became unacceptable.[38] Now that soldiers returned home from their service, society learned of the brutality men suffered at the hands of abusive officers but were helpless to do anything about it. Liberal civilian and military reformers under Alexander II advocated for a more respectful and humane relationship between officers and men. In an article directed at the officer corps, Miliutin wrote: "An army is not merely a physical force, a mass that serves as an instrument in military operations, but also an association of individuals endowed with intelligence and sensitivity."[39] He called on officers to respect and nurture these moral qualities. In the decades after emancipation, successive military codes made punishment more humane. The army established prisons in 1867 and penal battalions in 1878. New regulations in the 1870s forbade personal violence on the part of officers and NCOs, but enforcement was up to regiment commanders, many of whom disagreed with the softer approach. Corporal punishment was finally banned in 1904, and

The Officer Corps

personal violence against soldiers could land an NCO or officer in the guardhouse for up to six months. Finally, in 1906, with the adoption of a constitution, soldiers and their families had legal redress to abuse by officers.[40] Unsanctioned violence on the part of officers against soldiers resumed during the First World War. It became so prevalent that the term *kulachnuiu raspravu* (fist fight) was coined to describe it.

Treatment of soldiers improved dramatically because of the revolution. The change came about not so much because of the end of class differences between officers and men, but because of Marxist egalitarian ideology enforced by commissars who monitored officers' behavior and held them accountable for violations. Physical violence against soldiers virtually disappeared. Things began to change for the worse, however, in 1939 with the debacle that was the Soviet invasion of Finland. Mass indiscipline during and after the war led the Commissariat of Defense to issue Order No. 356 in October 1940. This order authorized officers to use physical force, including shooting soldiers, to maintain discipline. Given permission to manhandle or kill soldiers marked a shift in the outlook of officers toward their men.

In the post-war and post-Soviet periods, soldiers continued to be abused by their officers. Arkady Babchenko related his experience during the First Chechen War in 1996:

> What else can you expect of the officers if they themselves grew up in barracks? They too used to get beaten as cadets, and they still get beaten at their units. Every other colonel of ours is capable of little more than screaming and punching, reducing a lieutenant, captain or major to a moaning, disheveled wretch in front of junior ranks. Nor do the generals bother to mete out penalties to the colonels anymore, they simply hit them.[41]

Babchenko indicated the problem started with officers at the top whose example was followed by those below. Referring to his battalion commander:

> He treated us like cattle, talked down to us and used his fists a lot; he thought of us merely as cannon fodder, as drunks and

morons. "Dumb prick" was the Kombat's favorite expression, and indeed this was his favorite expression, and indeed this was the only way he addressed his infantry—"Hey you, dumb prick! Get over here!"—and then he'd smack you in the mouth with a "Take that!"[42]

Away from the fighting, treatment was no better. In 1998, a Lieutenant Logunov killed a soldier in a fit of anger. A military tribunal sentenced Logunov to seven years in prison, ignoring the soldier's family's and the military procurator's request for a longer sentence. A year earlier, to appease the public, Yeltsin appointed a new Military Procurator from outside the army. Iuri Dëmen, from the Federal Security Service, created a hotline for soldiers and their families to report abuse, and he sent teams around the country to conduct surprise inspections. In the first six months of 1998, they discovered 366 crimes against soldiers that commanders had covered up.[43]

Despite the army's efforts, officers continue to abuse solders into the Putin era. In 2003, courts-martial convicted 500 officers of physically abusing soldiers; 400 more were convicted in the first nine months of 2004. In 2005, a lieutenant, without hesitation, showed a journalist interviewing him a thirty-inch long, wooden baton that he used to punish unruly soldiers. He referred to it as an "educator."[44] Sadly, his attitude showed a reversion to the practices of the Imperial Russian Army, whose officers used the words "teach" and "beat" interchangeably.

Higher-ranking officers were just as prone to abuse soldiers. In 2014, Major Nikolai Chabanov beat a conscript named Alexei Snakin with a broom handle, forced him to wear a bulletproof vest and gas mask all day long, and then put Snakin "on a clock," telling him to buy a new computer for him. That night, Snakin committed suicide. A court-martial sentenced Chabanov merely to a suspended sentence. It took the intervention of human rights activists who publicized the case to have the major's sentence increased to three and a half years in a prison colony. Another officer, Colonel Doroshenko, deliberately withheld medical treatment from an ill soldier, which resulted in the man's death. Doroshenko was convicted and given four years in prison, but the sentence was annulled when it was discovered the statute of limitations had expired. Both these officers were reinstated to their positions and eventually promoted.[45] Though the Union of Committees of Soldiers' Mothers was often successful in having charges brought against officers for maltreatment of soldiers, sentences were routinely light or even suspended without deleterious effects on officers' careers, much to the mothers' ire.

Two heinous cases of hazing that occurred in 2005 highlight the gap between the public's desire for accountability and the officer corps' reluctance to change its behavior. At the Cheliabinsk Armor Academy, on New Year's Eve, a drunken officer beat private Andrei Sychov so seriously, and then encouraged a sergeant to continue beating him, that Sychov had to have his legs amputated and genitals surgically removed. Earlier, in April, in Moscow province, Private Vladimir Osetrov was beaten to death by three soldiers; his commander just ignored it. Only after Sychov's mother's successful efforts to publicize her son's case did Osetrov's mother make her case public, which caused the army to react. Several officers were arrested in each case. A poll taken one month after the stories broke revealed that 54 percent of the respondents disapproved of how the military functioned, up from 38 percent who disapproved in December 2005. Osetrov's mother, interviewed on national television, said, "I am facing a situation in which all ranks of the military and the prosecutors are fiercely defending the murderers as if they were their own sons."[46] She, like so many Russians at the time, expressed hope, but little faith, that the public outcry and military procurators' crusade against hazing would result in her son's attackers being punished. Her skepticism was not misplaced. In the midst of the outrage, the Minister of Defense, Sergei Ivanov, like the high command in the Soviet era, played down the incidents, blamed the ills of society in general, and offered cosmetic "solutions" that would in no way change business as usual in the units.[47] And yet two changes resulted from the outrage: the creation of Parents' Councils at all military bases that allowed for parents of soldiers to visit their sons and pass on any complaints; and the Public Chamber, a body of civilian employees within the Ministry of Defense that received complaints from soldiers' families outside the normal chain of command.[48]

The damage officer-brutality has done to the image and social standing of the officer corps is impossible to gauge. The fact that criminal cases are made public serves as a constant reminder that, as an institution, the officer corps is not morally superior to any other entity in Russian society. In 2003, for example, *Rossiiskaya gazeta* reported that "Almost a battalion of officers [was] sentenced for violence, with a general at the head and half of them [are now] behind bars." In 2005, 5,000 officers, including five generals, were convicted of crimes by courts-martial.[49]

Because officers treat soldiers the same today as they did three hundred years ago, it should be obvious that soldiers' hostile and untrusting attitudes toward them also have remained unchanged. On an ordinary basis, soldiers sought to keep their distance from officers to avoid trouble. Babchenko's and his comrades' attitudes in the 1990s were "we don't give a damn about the officers and will screw them over at every opportunity."[50] They referred to officers as jackals, just as soldiers did before the Revolution. All this is known to civilian society through newspaper articles, soldiers' letters, social media, and in direct conversation with demobilized soldiers.

When pushed too far, soldiers murder officers. In wartime, soldiers take the opportunity of combat to murder their officers. There is evidence that soldiers have murdered officers in every war Russia has fought since the emancipation. Babchenko, a veteran of the first Chechen War gives the explanation that has resonated for more than 160 years: "To shoot a swine of an officer in the back is in our eyes not a wicked deed but simple retribution. Swine shouldn't live when decent people die."[51] In peacetime, soldiers often wait until they can access weapons, often when practicing marksmanship at the firing range. In 2019, conscript soldier private Ramil Shamsutdinov shot to death, Senior Lt. Piankov along with seven other soldiers. Shamsutdinov had been hazed and was threatened with imminent rape. At his trial, covered by the national media, he claimed that he meant to kill six of the victims but was sorry he had shot the seventh unintentionally. He showed no remorse for killing the five soldiers and especially not the lieutenant who had condoned the hazing.[52]

More evidence indicating little to no change in officers' attitudes toward their subordinates is that officers have taken advantage of the

The Officer Corps

Ukraine war to exploit their men. Soldiers claim there is a system of bribes, in which they can buy themselves "wounds," leaves, rotation off the front lines, or permission to be excused from combat. In some units, all the soldiers contribute money to give generals multi-million-dollar bribes so that the whole unit can be kept away from the front. A Russian officer from a motorized rifle unit confirmed that soldiers can buy a "shell shock" wound with hospitalization for 10,000 to 50,000 dollars, depending on the rank of the soldier and on which sector of the front he is located. Leaves cost from five to ten thousand dollars and transfer from an active sector of the front to a quiet sector or early rotation home, 500 to 3,000 dollars. Because of social media, this type of corruption is well known among the civilian population and tarnishes the image of the officer corps.[53]

In summary, the main problem undermining the officer corps' relationship with the enlisted ranks and society, grows out of officers' resistance to accountability and a persisting attitude of social superiority. While the officers have always accepted that they were accountable to their superiors and to the head of state, they, to this day, reject being held accountable for their behavior by civil society and their men. As a result, society distrusts the officer corps. In the late twentieth and early twenty-first centuries, civil society and the soldiers have increasingly, and mostly unsuccessfully, tried to force the army to accept criticism and responsibility for maltreatment of the men and abuse of their positions, and to accept oversight from private civic groups and families. The result is that, since the modernization of Russian society, which began with the emancipation of the serfs, the Russian people generally have not held the officer corps in as high regard as the officers hold themselves.

CHAPTER 4
SOCIETY, THE MILITARY, AND THE STATE

As the preceding chapters have illustrated, for centuries, the Russian people have had and still have an ambivalent relationship with their army. This chapter examines the interrelationship between society, the military, and the state in the context of competing visions and expectations, those of the state and the army versus those of society. It argues that as long as Russia has authoritarian systems of government, these relationships will be fraught. Two major themes emerge in the pages ahead: the state's attempts to use patriotism, loyalty, and service to militarize society from the early twentieth century; and the people's resistance to militarization. From the inception of the imperial period under Peter I, the state has equated military service with loyalty to the regime. Since the turn of the nineteenth century, the state, to further its militarization agenda, has employed the education system to conduct patriotic education, sponsor militarized youth groups, and conduct pre-induction military training courses. Until the twentieth century, the state had cared little about the attitude of its subjects toward service because compliance to conscription was high and resistance, though persistent, was low in absolute terms. The army's attitude changed with the loss of the Russo-Japanese War in 1905, which the leadership blamed on the soldiers' lack of patriotism. Since then, successive regimes have shown a remarkable consistency in attempting to convince the population that military service is a patriotic act. They have done so in such a way as not only to secure manpower and loyal service, but also to legitimize and bolster the authoritarian nature of the regime. Society's response has been decidedly mixed and increasingly oppositional over time, as demonstrated by rising tolerance of draft evasion, emergence of anti-war movements, and attempts by wives and mothers to hold the army accountable for its treatment of soldiers. Since the beginning of the Putin era in 2000, a culture war between Western-inspired liberal internationalism and more traditional nationalism and Russian xenophobia has pitted much of the younger, liberal generation against the older conservative generation.

Defining the terms militarism, militarization, and patriotism is essential to making the argument that despite ongoing efforts, the Russian state has failed to militarize society. Militarism, militarization, and patriotism are imprecise terms that can mean different things to different people and are complex sets of mentalities and behaviors that can pull nations and people in different directions depending on the issues, eras, and political environments. I employ M. V. Naidu's description that militarism consists of attitudinal and behavioral elements such as moral values, behavior patterns, and emotions that states can use to construct propagandistic narratives that present military capability as the most meaningful and effective instrument for achieving any or all national goals, and that soldiers, weapons, and wars are the most necessary and noble tools for national defense and international advancement.[1] Militarism is, in this view, an "ism" adopted by the state. Some elements of militarism manifest in Russia over the last three centuries include: an excessive emphasis on military ceremonies; ideologies supportive of military ideals (feudalism, communism, ultra-nationalism); disproportionately heavy state expenditure for military purposes; the state's willingness to bear inordinately high casualties in warfare; readiness to the point of eagerness to commit the armed forces in foreign and domestic conflicts; and extensive controls over life for military purposes.[2] A militarized state, however, is not the equivalent of a militarized society. The above definitions of militarism focus on state institutions and ignore the agency of people and their ability to reject or independently interpret the state's messaging and to oppose it and act in their self-interest. Militarization, it follows, is the process by which the state attempts to convince society to accept militarism.[3]

The working definition of patriotism employed herein comes from Johanna Dahlin who writes: "Patriotic loyalty is associative, based on community, a loyalty based on the role of the individual

Society, the Military, and the State

and the state and its institutions. There is supposed to be mutuality between the duties of the citizen and the state." Dahlin argues that the Russian state in many ways has been seen as unjust and has not fulfilled its obligations to its citizens, who can therefore question their obligation to the state. Furthermore, patriotism can be a loyalty that while locally based, extends beyond current politics to include the wider community of compatriots and calls "on essentialist values such as naturalness, home, and family."[4] The upshot is that, though the state may control the official narrative defining Imperial Russian/Soviet/Russian patriotism, Russians have used their agency to define patriotism for themselves sometimes in opposition to the state's.

The State's Vision of How Society Should Relate to Military Service

The ways in which the state wants the population to relate to the army and military service has evolved over the centuries. From Peter I to Nicholas II, the state saw military service for the lower classes primarily in utilitarian terms, not caring much about how the people felt about it as long as they acknowledged their obligation to serve when called. Military service was seldom deemed a patriotic duty; instead, the regime's "Orthodoxy, Autocracy, and Nationality," credo, created by Nicholas I, was meant to define the objects of loyalty, well aware that, because it was a multinational, multiethnic, and multi-confessional empire, a significant number of people would be deaf to it. Not until the brief constitutional period, 1906–14, when the tsar, though still the commander-in-chief, was no longer an autocrat, did the army link patriotism with service.

During the Soviet period, 1917–91, the state used military service to create a space for feelings of allegiance to the regime—still a multiethnic, multinational empire. In the years before the Second World War, service, although still compulsory, was promoted as a privilege, one denied to class enemies such as former nobles, the bourgeoisie, and wealthy peasants. The regime equated service with loyalty to the ideals of the October Revolution, the Soviet state, and Communist Party rule.

Social History of the Russians and Their Army

After the war, the state toned down revolutionary idealism and focused more on service as a duty and obligation.

In the immediate post-Soviet period under President Boris Yeltsin, the state downplayed military service. Beginning in 2000, President Vladimir Putin's regime began a campaign, which continues to this day, to equate military service with patriotism, and patriotism with nationalism to increase compliance with conscription and to recruit volunteers. Putin encourages military service as the primary way to demonstrate loyalty to the state, which essentially means supporting him and his political agenda.[5]

Popular Associations of Military Service with Patriotism

Russians' ability to define patriotism for themselves and to understand their interests as separate from the state have been the fundamental challenges of the various regimes' attempts to impose their definitions of patriotism and to associate them with military service. No matter what definition the state or military gave to patriotism, people have defined patriotism and what it calls them to do for themselves. Some have agreed with and conformed to the official interpretation, and some have completely rejected it. Ultra-right imperialists and Russian nationalists typically have agreed with the state's version of patriotism: loyalty and service to the existing political and social order. Meanwhile, many on the left have argued for liberal reform of the state or for revolution to destroy it. They have done so while professing a genuine love for Russia and loathing for the army, which they consider a repressive tool of the state. For non-Russian minorities, the state's version of patriotism often rang hollow; they saw themselves as peoples conquered by Russia. Their identities as non-Russians heightened resistance to the Russification programs of the late tsarist and Soviet periods, programs that drew attention to their national or ethnic identities.

From the early nineteenth century, patriotism was a concept demonstrated mainly by the educated elite; it did not become meaningful to the common people until later in the century. For serfs

Society, the Military, and the State

and the empire's colonized minorities, local identity was stronger than any affiliation with the state or its institutions and certainly not with the army. The idea of the nation and people's place in it began to take root after the emancipation of the serfs and the gradual modernization of Russia through education, literacy, urbanization, and the growth of civic participation in the public sphere. Over the ensuing decades, the concept of citizenship grew, along with the sense that military service ought to be one of reciprocal obligations: If the people owe the state military service, then the state owes the people for performing it. Although the state rejected the idea of reciprocity, people's expectations of the state became a factor in determining popular devotion and loyalty. This concept carried over into the Soviet era and into the present.

More thoughtful Russians have rejected state-supplied definitions of patriotism, reserving the right to establish their own understanding of nationalism and patriotism. They are keenly aware of the difference between loyalty to the state and patriotism for Russia. Their distinctions allow for a patriot to be opposed to the state and military service. Proponents of this view acknowledge the tension between "homeland" and "state," pointing to the emotional connotations of the word *rodina*, which can be both national and local, with loyalty to the country taking precedence over loyalty to the state. This thinking allows for the primary duty of a good patriot to be—to contribute to what the individual perceives to be the correct development of the country. Patriotism that is anchored in family and community is often perceived as detached from the state, often regarded as a corrupt bureaucracy bound by red tape.[6] This understanding first enabled tens of thousands and then millions of Russians and subject peoples—elites and commoners—from the Decembrist revolt in 1825 to the present, to adopt radical or reformist goals and behavior to change the system, even violently, out of love for Russia and to identify as patriots while evading military service.

Since 2000, use of the word patriotism has become ubiquitous in Putin's political discourse. Many Russians understand that the regime is trying to use its version of patriotism to manipulate them. Some derisively label a person who crosses the line from healthy love of

Social History of the Russians and Their Army

homeland to unhealthy pro-Putin chauvinism as a "*kvasnoi* patriot" (super-patriot) or *ura*-patriot (a hurrah-shouting patriot). In 2022, anti-war Russians came up with a new pejorative term, "Z-patriot," for those ostentatiously displaying the pro-war Z symbol. Many Russians, without referencing the military, define themselves as "true" patriots in contrast to the *ura*-patriots, whom they see as superficial. The war with Ukraine, the acid test of Putin's patriotic trope, has brought the culture war into families. Skeptics among the younger generation have assigned the pejorative nickname "*vatnik*" to people—including their parents—whom they see as being emotionally trapped in the past and willfully ignorant of the unjust nature of Putin's domestic and foreign policies. Such parents see their children as unpatriotic at best and traitors at worst.[7]

Regime Attempts to Militarize Society

Under Nicholas II, the regime began a campaign to militarize society, a campaign that was continued by the Soviet Union, discarded in the 1990s, and then resurrected by Putin. The purpose of militarization is to bolster the political and social power of the state over the people. The decision to relate patriotism to military service and to use the education system as the primary vehicle to militarize society by indoctrinating youth grew out of Russia's loss of the Russo-Japanese War (1904–5). The defeat spurred the army high command to investigate what had gone wrong, but rather than examine its own faults, the high command, with no evidence whatsoever, concluded that soldiers' lack of patriotism led to defeat. Acknowledging that the masses had agency and could choose to serve loyally or not, along with the idea that people could be taught to be patriotic, represented a sea change in elite attitudes and a watershed in Russian societal-military relations. This new concern about popular attitudes then led, in 1909, to the introduction of patriotic curricula in the public schools and the creation of paramilitary youth groups. Educators, army officers, and veterans used military drills, gymnastics, patriotic instruction, and youth participation in imperial celebrations to shape positive attitudes toward the monarch, the Fatherland, and military service.[8]

Patriotic Education in the Schools

Not until after the emancipation of the serfs did Russia's Ministry of Education begin educating the people in earnest. It established a national curriculum in which the watchwords, "Orthodoxy, Autocracy, and Nationality" served as the basis for patriotic instruction. Slack oversight of teachers and local administrators enabled liberal- and radical-minded teachers to present anti-autocratic views and to frame patriotism in terms unfavorable to the regime. Such views were especially pronounced in the many private schools not subject to government oversight. Universities were rife with anti-regime sentiment among both students and professors who rejected the autocracy's simplistic watchwords as a basis for patriotism. Because of the royal family's close relationship to the army, this rejection of autocracy was simultaneously a rejection of militarism. With the rise of revolutionary movements, campuses became so radical that Alexander II closed all institutions of higher education for a year in 1862. Many students who went on to become teachers espoused a love for Russia that need not be reflected in military service or loyalty to the tsar.

With Nicholas II's enthusiastic support, the army offered to teach gymnastics and military drill to school children. Local regiments took the lead in providing instructors to schools in towns, villages, and cities in their vicinity. Relying largely on active-duty units, such instruction was unevenly distributed across the empire. Because the military-patriotic education of youth only began five years before the outbreak of the First World War and had not spread far beyond the major cities, it is impossible to know what effect it had on people's willingness to serve in the army.

Following the Bolshevik seizure of power in October 1917, the entirety of the Soviet period was one of a gradual attempt by the state to militarize society, primarily at the behest of the military, to a degree only imagined by the tsarist regimes. Shortly after the civil war, the

Bolshevik state began a program to militarize youth in the schools through patriotic education, political indoctrination, and school-based, party-affiliated organizations such as the Little Octobrists for elementary-age children, Young Pioneers for middle- and high-school-aged youth, and the Komsomol (Leninist Youth League) for older teens and youth up to age thirty. During the 1920s and 1930s, the indoctrination efforts of these organizations focused on the heroic acts of soldiers and partisans during the October Revolution and civil war, with the intent to help young people see military service, patriotism, and loyalty as a unified trinity. The final step in militarizing youth was taken in the 1960s when the army assigned uniformed officers and soldiers to teach military skills in mandatory pre-induction training classes in the schools. Teachers were encouraged to invite the veterans of the Second World War to present "Lessons in Courage." Also in the 1960s, the state launched a massive program to build monuments to the Great Patriotic War that emphasized military service and sacrifice as the highest order of Soviet patriotism.[9]

During the Yeltsin years, Communist Party-affiliated youth groups were disbanded. Pre-induction military instruction was abolished and replaced with health and life skills classes. Schools were in disarray as the Ministry of Education rewrote the patriotic content of history lessons to downplay the Soviet era, examine its faults, and de-emphasize military heroics. Instead, a more holistic view of Russian history was attempted.

Within months of becoming president in 2000, and urged by the military, Putin began to emphasize military-centric patriotic education. He launched the first of four military-patriotic educational five-year plans in 2001. Putin apparently agreed with his generals that the difficulties in military recruitment were due to a lack of patriotism in society, so his regime turned to the school system to teach that military service was an integral, if not foundational, aspect of patriotism. The aim of patriotic education was to create a shared understanding of patriotism, a positive image of the armed forces, and to protect the moral health of youth that was, according to the deputy chief of the General Staff, Lt. Gen. Iuri Tuchkov, subject to "external ideological attacks by Russia's opponents," with their "alien views, morals and customs."[10] The XIV World Russian People's Council in the summer of 2010 concluded

Society, the Military, and the State

that patriotic education was necessary to save Russian youth saying, "Only through the united efforts of all the forces of society can we resist the sin and vices that are being deliberately implanted in our society today from outside and inside the country," and only such education can safeguard youth from "the lust and debauchery of the street."[11] In July 2014, at a meeting of government officials, Putin, echoed the army's opinion, stating that ramping up patriotic content in the schools was designed to increase voluntary military recruitment by cultivating the value of national service. Putin's understanding of patriotism and "love for the Motherland" is bound to ideas of citizenship and sacred duty; and sacred duty translates to military service.[12]

In 2014, in a bid to further militarize public education, the Ministry of Defense encouraged high schools to create cadet classes. Schools, on a voluntary basis, created separate classes for students considering military careers. In addition to the regular education curriculum, cadets learn how to march, how to disassemble and assemble machine guns, and marksmanship. Student cadets are distinguished from ordinary students by wearing military uniforms. By September 2022, 730 of the 36,248 eligible schools had founded cadet classes, more than one-third of which were in Moscow.

Since Putin became president, commemorating events of Russia's military history have become a prominent aspect of the school year. In the 1980s, the only public commemoration of the Great Patriotic War was on Victory Day, but since Putin's third five-year plan for patriotic education, the school calendar became increasingly crowded with mandatory patriotic events. In addition to Victory Day, children celebrate the Day of Remembrance of the Victims of the Blockade (of Leningrad) every September; in November they remember select military conflicts as part of the Day of Military Glory; and in February they participate in events dedicated to Defender of the Fatherland Day.[13] The Soviet-era "Lessons of Courage" program was resurrected with talks to school children delivered by veterans of the wars in Afghanistan, Chechnya, and Ukraine.

In 2022, Putin ordered that every Monday morning before regular classes started, students would assemble to observe the raising of the Russian flag and sing the national anthem, followed by a class called

Social History of the Russians and Their Army

"Important Conversations." The Ministry of Education provided patriotic curricula for these "conversations." According to the ministry, these lessons are to assist in "protecting Russian society from destructive information and psychological impact," and to "strengthen traditional Russian spiritual and moral values." In fact, the content is unmistakably intended to generate support for the war in Ukraine among children as young as kindergarten age.

Officially Sponsored Military-Patriotic Youth Groups

The military's attempt to popularize military service and to link it to patriotism through locally run youth groups originated in 1909, when the Russian state and military sponsored military-patriotic youth groups to promote loyalty and make military service attractive. In 1910, besides teaching gymnastics in the public schools, the army officially accepted responsibility for sponsoring extracurricular co-educational school-based *poteshnyi* (scout) units. Most *poteshnyi* units limited themselves to teaching gymnastics and drill, but some also provided more directly useful military skills such as map reading, marksmanship, and infantry tactics. Girls were directed to stereotypical gender roles including nursing but were also included in gymnastics. Retired, reserve, and active-duty officers volunteered to found and supervise these units. In addition to gymnastics and drill, instructors usually delivered lectures and readings that promoted loyalty to the tsar and Fatherland. For high school-aged youth, the army sponsored co-ed *sokol* (falcon) clubs that focused on gymnastics. The tsar and the royal family took a particular interest in the *poteshnyi* and *sokol* clubs and welcomed them to their various estates to perform drills and gymnastics.[14]

In the years following the civil war, the Bolsheviks copied the tsarist regime in creating voluntary militarized extracurricular youth groups in the form of the Society of Friends of Defense, Aviation-Chemical Construction (OSOAVIAKHIM), to teach youth military skills such as marksmanship, parachuting, first aid, and glider piloting, hoping to interest them in military service. Sports and gymnastics were also

Society, the Military, and the State

an important component of Osoaviakhim. Just as during the tsarist era, girls were allowed to join even though they were not expected to serve. The Commissariat of Defense associated the military preparation of youth with the inculcation of Soviet patriotism. In their thinking, military service was the essential manifestation of patriotism and masculinity, which combined to produce the ideal Soviet man. The association of military service and patriotism with manhood (a holdover from the tsarist era) gradually became accepted by much of Soviet society. The military supported Osoaviakhim with equipment, weapons, and advisors, but it was up to local civilian authorities to organize the groups. By 1935, about 2.5 million boys and girls, in their after-school hours, had earned the badge "Prepared for Labor and Defense," and hundreds of thousands earned badges for marksmanship and horsemanship. In May 1941, 13 million youth from school children to college students were participating in Osoaviakhim activities.[15] The Soviet state disbanded Osoaviakhim during the Second World War but revived and reorganized it in 1948, and in 1951 renamed it the All-Union Voluntary Society for Assistance to the Army, Air Force, and Navy (DOSAAF).

Parallel to state-sponsored militarized youth groups was the Communist Party-sponsored Komsomol noted above. From the late 1920s to the outbreak of war in 1939, military activities began to occupy more and more Komsomol work. The IX Congress of the Komsomol, held in January 1931, resolved that youth who had not undergone military training had no place in the ranks of the Komsomol.[16] Russian scholars Olga Galkova and Irina Petrova concluded that, from the earliest days, the Bolsheviks' militarization of youth was firmly connected with the practice of socialist construction. Its main goals were not only the comprehensive preparation of the young generation for military service, "but also a high degree of intertwining of state, military, and public interests, leading to the identification by young people with the state's interests of strengthening the country's defense capability and socialist construction as their own, personal interests."[17] While this was likely the intent, its success must be heavily qualified because the outreach to youth was mostly limited to the urban areas leaving millions of peasant youth untouched.

Figure 4.1 Russian youth participating in military summer camp. iStock photos.

In the Putin era, DOSAAF lives on as DOSAAF Russia and serves the same purpose of inculcating patriotism, strengthening the moral and physical health of youth, and preparing them for military service. Another youth organization, The All-Russian Military-Patriotic Movement "*Iunarmiia*" (Youth Army), an organization under the Russian Movement of Children and Youth, sponsored by the Ministry of Defense in conjunction with the Ministry of Education, is affiliated with military units, military schools, DOSAAF Russia, and the Central Sports Club of the Army (Figure 4.1).[18] Founded in 2016, this organization recruits in the public schools and is open to boys and girls ages eight to seventeen (Figure 4.2). In some ways it is a rebranding of the Komsomol—which its founders and supporters evince nostalgia for—with Russian nationalism replacing communism as the core ideology.

Iunarmiia's two main purposes are to be a pipeline for volunteers for the army, and to instill "Russianness" by reaffirming traditional gender roles and inspiring self-sacrifice, humility, hard work, and the pursuit of heroism. The oath of the *Iunarmiia* includes a promise that its members will prepare themselves to serve the Fatherland.

Society, the Military, and the State

Figure 4.2 *Iunarmiia* youth marching in the annual Victory Day parade. iStock photos.

According to the code of the movement, the honor and glory of Russia are the highest values youth can strive for. *Iunarmiia*'s official song is "You and I are destined to serve Russia." The leadership of the movement considers patriotic education to be a means to save youth from criminality, alcohol, drugs, and the pernicious influence of television and social media. In September 2024, *Iunarmiia* claimed to have 1.6 million members equaling 7 percent of eligible youth. The Ministry of Defense is convinced of the need for more thorough military-patriotic indoctrination to combat pacifist sentiments in youth, believing that pacifism encourages draft evasion and hinders recruitment.[19]

Pre-Induction Military Training

Despite forty years of work by the public schools and the Komsomol, in the 1960s, the military perceived apolitical attitudes among "self-indulgent youth" whose loyalty they considered questionable. The army leadership, looking through a Marxist Cold War lens, imagined that the unmilitary outlook of teenagers had led to decadent morals, materialism, and pacifism. They blamed Western propaganda broadcasts by the Voice of America, Radio Free Europe, BBC World Service, and commercial radio and television broadcasts from Western Europe widely, though illegally accessed by teenagers. The officers' world view would seem to indicate that they thought militarized patriotism was the norm and that Russia's youth had been led astray rather than the opposite, that the majority of teens might naturally be disinterested in going off to the military. In 1967, the Brezhnev regime acquiesced to the urging of the Ministry of Defense to establish mandatory pre-induction military training (*nachal'noi voennoi podgotovki*—NVP) in the schools, hoping it would remedy the situation by instilling military values in youth. The curricula spanned two school years for a total of 140 hours of instruction that directly linked the idea of military service with patriotic education. To further militarize youth, the Ministry of Defense sponsored semi-mandatory militarized activities that included war games: "Summer lightning" (for male and female youth ages ten to fifteen years) and "Zarnitsa" (for ages sixteen to eighteen). These involved youth interacting with military units throughout the year and summer camps that were essentially militarized week-long games of capture the flag involving small-unit tactics, live fire with weapons, first aid, and other military tasks supervised by soldiers.

NVP ceased with the collapse of communism, but in 2014, Putin's proxy war with Ukraine led directly to an increase in the intensity of military-patriotic indoctrination and militarized outreach to prepare youth for military service, enhance their patriotic feelings, and counteract "decadent" influences. In autumn 2022, the national curriculum for public schools was changed to add more nationalist patriotic content, and in spring 2023, mandatory NVP was reinstated for both male and female 10th and 11th graders. This training, as in the Soviet period, included military drill, the use of personal protective equipment, small arms and hand grenades, and first aid. Students learned small unit tactics, the composition and armament of a motorized rifle squad and its infantry fighting vehicle, and how to construct individual fighting positions. As in the Soviet period, veterans, reservists, and retirees are the instructors. Time during the school day for this instruction comes at the expense of the health education and life skills program. Indicative of the regime's seriousness in militarizing youth is its robbing from education to fund NVP. The Ministry of Education was forced to divert billions of rubles intended to buy supplies and equipment for chemistry, biology, physics, and computer science instruction to pay for it.[20]

Societal Response and Resistance to Militarization

The popular response to the successive regimes' attempts to militarize society has been mixed. During the tsarist era, the nobility generally accepted that voluntary military service as officers was a way to manifest loyalty to the tsar, but they also displayed self-serving motivations such as seeing it simply as employment or to enhance their social standing. Men of the lower classes saw conscripted service as obedience to the law, not a manifestation of patriotism. Socialists and revolutionaries preached anti-militarism, and liberals were sympathetic to anti-military thought and rhetoric. Service during the Soviet period was seen as an inevitable burden not associated with support for the state and was avoided by those who had the means to do so. The post-Soviet period has seen the highest levels of anti-military activity and anti-militarism in Russia's history.

Anti-War Movements and Protests, and Tolerance of Service Avoidance

Taking an anti-war stance is one way the Russian peoples have responded to state militarism. Though there were always people who were against Russia's wars, to characterize their opposition as movements until late in the twentieth century is rather difficult due to successful police repression, low levels of literacy, and lack of mass communications. Opposition was largely local, individual, and unorganized. Many times, anti-war activities were more about resisting the government than war. In the nineteenth century, the radical left and liberal reformers combined protests of the Crimean War, then the Russo-Turkish War of 1877–8, with attacks on autocracy through pamphlets and in illegal discussion groups.[21] During both the Russo-Japanese War and the First World War, anti-war sentiments were openly expressed within elite circles, not only by those who were against the war and the autocracy, but also by those who favored autocratic rule. As in previous wars, liberals and revolutionaries were against both the war and the regime. Between 1914 and 1917, the revolutionary political parties sowed doubt about the tsarist government's war aims and then successfully undermined the liberal Provisional Government in 1917 with their anti-war agitation.[22] Rather than anti-war voices during the Second World War, one heard defeatist voices that hoped a Soviet loss to the Axis would lead to the downfall of the Stalinist regime.

The Soviet Union's war in Afghanistan elicited opposition immediately on the individual level. People put up anti-war placards and graffitied public places. Such activists were genuinely against the war and the communist regime's pervasive militarism. The secret police tracked down and jailed many. Prominent persons who spoke out against the war, such as Andrei Sakharov, were fired from their jobs and sent into internal exile. Once Gorbachev introduced *glasnost* in 1986, people began to protest the war without fear of arrest and the media began to question it. In 1989, 31 percent of people polled expressed opposition to the war.[23] Those who supported Gorbachev's reforms were usually also against the war and militarism.

The two wars in Chechnya, 1994–6 and 1999–2009, led to the creation of what can legitimately be labeled anti-war movements, but with distinct anti-militarist and political agendas as well. The First Chechen War began in November 1994, and on January 3, 1995, the Union of Committees of Soldiers' Mothers held their first anti-war vigil on Red-Square in Moscow in which they commemorated the soldiers killed in Chechnya. Three days later, a group of mothers led by Maria Kirbasova went to Grozny, Chechnya, to confront Russian generals to get their sons, first-year conscripts, transferred from the war zone where they had been illegally assigned. The mothers succeeded, in part due to media coverage. Later, in February, the CSM began holding small anti-war protests in Moscow in conjunction with other anti-war groups. Then, in March, about 100 CSM mothers began a trek from Moscow's Red Square to Grozny gathering support along the way to protest the war and raise anti-war awareness. In Chechnya, they discovered that the Soviet Army had committed atrocities, mainly the killing of women and children, which they then publicized.[24] Many consider the mothers' actions and the exposure of the atrocities to have been key in turning much of Russian society against the conflict and creating sufficient pressure on Boris Yeltsin to negotiate an end to the war.

In February 2022, in the wake of the Ukraine invasion, the regime, on Putin's orders, outlawed virtually all humanitarian and nongovernmental organizations, not to mention public protests. Still, tens of thousands of Russians found ways to protest the war. Large street protests in the capital and St. Petersburg in February and March 2022 and again in September 2023 were crushed by overwhelming police forces. Simultaneously, people carried out individual anti-war acts. The more than 24,000 members of the "Feminist Anti-War Resistance" posted anti-war leaflets in public places and held protest messages on pickets. On March 8, 2022, International Women's Day, they succeeded in getting tens of thousands of female activists to leave flowers on monuments where they held minutes-long silent vigils to commemorate the deaths of Ukrainian civilians. Besides being against the war, they were and remain politically opposed to Putin.[25] Anti-war activists perpetrated scores of arson attacks on military commissariats across Russia and sabotaged hundreds of railroad switch boxes. Others joined local annual May Day parades carrying anti-war signs. Human rights activist Yuri Terekhov identified 263 anti-war groups and initiatives within and without Russia eighteen months into the war consisting of 108 protest diaspora organizations with contacts inside Russia; sixty-five activist-to-activist projects that aid Russians to emigrate to avoid the war, help men avoid mobilization, and provide legal and psychological support; thirty new anti-Putin independent media outlets; thirty-seven peaceful political resistance organizations of youths, feminists, and street-level "guerrilla" groups; ten violent and armed resistance organizations; and thirteen anti-war art projects.[26]

Social History of the Russians and Their Army

On Russia's Mothers' Day, November 27, 2022, the "Feminist Anti-war Resistance" movement and an organized group of mothers of mobilized and contract soldiers issued an open letter to the State Duma and Russian Federation Council in which they demanded an end to the war and the withdrawal of Russian troops from Ukraine. They argued that the government should instead be spending more to help women and children.[27] On the first anniversary of the war's beginning, anti-war protests were held in at least fourteen cities. By this time, nearly 20,000 people—almost half of whom were women— had been detained for anti-war activity, and the number of convictions for anti-war acts increased monthly. Eighteen months into the war, courts had tried more than 8,000 cases of "discrediting the army." The severity of the prison sentences also increased from an average of two years in 2022 to five in mid-2023.[28] That people were still willing to protest the war by whatever means possible speaks to the depth and breadth of their anti-militarism and opposition to the regime that promotes and relies on it.

Toleration of Draft Evasion/Service Avoidance

Even though Russian society has generally recognized the legitimacy of the draft, many people have been sympathetic to peacetime draft evasion. During the imperial period, families aided their men's attempts to be disqualified from the draft, paid bribes, or facilitated flight to escape it. In the Soviet period, especially during the 1950s, 1960s, and late 1980s, many citizens and national minorities approved of draft evasion. In 1988, 40 percent of conscripts' families claimed they did not view military service as honorable. In both 1998 and 1999, RIA-Novosti polls revealed that 56 percent of respondents viewed the military negatively.[29] Between 1997 and 2007, no more than 35 percent of respondents supported conscription in an annual Levada Center poll, whereas, in 2006, 53 percent condoned draft evasion and in 2014 the numbers of those expressing anti-draft sentiments reached 61 percent, before falling to 23 percent in 2017 after three years of Russian-supported conflict in the Donbas and an uptick in nationalist propaganda.[30] The shift in popular attitudes seems to have

Society, the Military, and the State

been temporary. With the February 2022 invasion of Ukraine, tens of thousands of draft-aged men and reservists fled the country to avoid being called up, often with the support of friends and family.

Protest Against Patriotic Education and Militarized Indoctrination of Youth

Another reaction to the state's attempt to militarize society was to protest patriotic education and militarized indoctrination of youth. There is no record of opposition to the introduction of patriotic education in the late tsarist era nor to the founding of *poteshnyi* and *sokol* clubs. Given that those programs had begun less than a decade before the outbreak of the First World War, were on a small scale, and tsarist censorship obstructed any criticism of regime-supported initiatives, it is unsurprising.

Because the USSR was a police state, it was impossible for parents in the Soviet era to object to the military-patriotic curriculum or to NVP. Although officially a student had to finish the entire 140-hour NVP program to graduate and advance to higher education, educators were slack in enforcing it. Directors of schools who had other priorities or disagreed with the idea of militarization in principle, often ignored both NVP and DOSAAF and left the instructors to their own devices while committing as few resources as possible.[31] The fact that NVP fell away almost immediately following the end of communist rule indicates the lack of societal support for it.

The reintroduction of NVP in 2023 generated a mixed response. Some parents, who had undergone NVP training in their youth, thought it had been a waste of time and did not want their children subjected to it. Many teachers objected, and independent teachers' unions called imposing NVP "madness." They argued that "the continued militarization of everyday life 'destroys' the education process."[32] While clearly an extreme reaction, it is notable that teachers' unions identified NVP as militarism and opposed it.

When the Ministry of Education announced in summer 2022 that "Important Conversations" would begin in the fall, many teachers and parents were outraged at the blatant attempt, in their words, to "brainwash" and militarize children. Emphatic parent pushback against indoctrinating the youngest children succeeded in causing the Ministry of Education to temporarily drop the pro-war aspect of the lessons for kindergarteners through fourth graders. Anti-war, anti-Putin parents let their children skip the class, though zealous pro-Putin teachers and administrators sometimes brought pressure on the parents to cooperate. Still, many parents have frank talks with their children to challenge what schools teach. Liberal anti-Putin teachers ignore the government-provided materials and spend their time on other subjects, resign, or continue to resist until they are fired when denounced by pro-Putin teachers or parents.[33]

All indications are that this resistance continues today. Anti-Putin teachers resist propagandizing their students. A male teacher, a veteran of the Second Chechen war, who opposed the war with Ukraine, said about "Important Conversations," "The [anti-war] teacher just needs to read out of a training manual—which most do—automatically and without emotion, and then they discuss cool things with the children."[34] He, and many other teachers expressed skepticism that the state will succeed in brainwashing teenagers because teens already have a point of view—most are anti-war—and the little ones do not care because they have other, childhood interests. Another teacher's opinion was that because educators resent being poorly paid, they intentionally do a "half-assed job" in anything extra the government asks of them.[35] Some, however, are pro-Putin and go all out with the propaganda.

In general, a fundamental weakness of Putin's five-year plans of patriotic instruction, including "Important Conversations," is that how the message is conveyed is, like in the imperial period, almost totally in the hands of local school officials. Administrators and teachers who object to the Ministry of Education's materials, either ignore them, modify them, or teach something completely different. Parents resist the militarization of their children by putting them in private schools, of which there are thousands that do not fall under the authority of the Ministry of Education and do not have NVP. The teachers and administrators of these schools are largely pro-democracy and antimilitary in outlook.

Just as there are parents and teachers who object to the reintroduction of NVP and nationalist propaganda into schools, there are those who abhor *Iunarmiia* and other militarized youth organizations. Critics argue that *Iunarmiia* is less about patriotism to Russia and more about breeding loyalty to Putin, who, until 2021, faced competition from opposition politicians, including Alexei Navalny, who inspired teenagers to participate in anti-Putin street protests. Valentina Grebenik, executive secretary of the Union of Committees of Soldiers' Mothers of Russia, said of Putin's militaristic bent in 2019: "It's a crime. The militarization of childhood is banned by the [United Nations] Convention on the Rights of the Child. What is going on is an outrage against our kids and our society." Obviously, anti-Putin parents keep their sons and daughters out of *Iunarmiia*. Some have compared the *Iunarmiia*, to the Hitler Youth.[36]

Mothers' and Wives' Activities to Hold the Army Accountable

On June 28, 2022, thirty wives of Buriat soldiers staged a protest demanding that their husbands be sent home from the war in Ukraine and posted a video of it on YouTube.[37] This, and other public protests by wives and mothers outraged by Russia's invasion of Ukraine, was just the latest in Russian society's fairly recent bid to resist militarization by holding the army accountable for the men it takes. Some resistance surfaced during the First World War but lapsed with the Revolution. In the USSR, no one dared openly protest mandatory military service or its consequences for families until the late 1980s. Neither did anyone challenge the army's right to treat soldiers with cruelty, indifference, or to allow an environment of brutality to pervade their service. Until the Chechen wars, people did not openly criticize the army for its profligate waste of soldiers' lives. The various ways in which the Russian people have sought to hold the military establishment accountable suggests that Russian society does not blindly support the military.

Until Russia adopted its first constitution (The Fundamental Laws) in 1906, people had no legal way to hold the army accountable, and no means existed for the masses to use public opinion to pressure the government. The Fundamental Laws enabled people, through their State Duma representatives, to voice complaints against the military for the hardships it imposed on families (which resulted in the establishment of monthly stipends, *paika*, in 1912, and pensions for men discharged due to injury) and its abuses of the men. During the Soviet period, prior to *glasnost*, the armed forces were above public reproach. Mothers protesting hazing and the war in Afghanistan in the 1980s and public questioning of the need for conscription represented a watershed in the history of Russian society-military relations. Predictably, the army resisted attempts to hold it accountable and denied there were any problems in the ranks. The high command insisted that universal military obligation was essential for national defense and insinuated that anti-war protesters were disloyal. Public discussion of hazing tarnished the image of the army, and draft evasion took on a national character. Ever since the Gorbachev era, the Russian people—led by women—have done their best to hold the army accountable for its care of their men, and sympathy is widespread for those who wish to avoid service.

Mothers of soldiers emerged as a social interest group determined to hold the government and army accountable. As noted in Chapter 1, the first organized challenge to the army's treatment of soldiers began in 1989 with the creation of the Committee of Soldiers' Mothers. The CSM confronted military authorities at all levels, from regiments to the Ministry of Defense. Originally created to protest hazing, the CSM's activities grew to include the defense of soldiers' rights, which were violated in a variety of ways. After the disintegration of the USSR, the Union of Committees of Soldiers' Mothers of Russia (UCSMR) at its peak had 300 branches throughout the Russian Federation. The UCSMR solicited donations from its members, the public, and local governments. It used the funds to establish rehabilitation centers for soldiers who left the army for health reasons and to lobby legislators. Soon, its efforts expanded to include educating conscripts, their parents, and wives on soldiers' legal rights. The UCSMR educated mothers about how to make individual complaints when military leaders violated their sons' rights. Through its regional and local chapters, the UCSMR instituted regular inspections of military units and organized public protests. At the national level, with the assistance of sympathetic law makers, mothers initiated legislative proposals to require the military to improve the conditions of service.

The UCSMR became internationally recognized, and its head, Valentina Melnikova, spoke before the United States Helsinki Commission in 2004 to publicize the group's efforts to end the Russian military's abuse of soldiers. She stated that the UCSMR's larger goals were military reform, abolition of conscription, the establishment of a professional armed force, and the expansion of civilian control over the military. Its political agenda was explicitly pro-democracy. Its members believed that only democracy could deliver a humane army and end the "legal slavery, chaos, and corruption at all levels of the Russian military."[38] More worrisome for the army and Putin than the challenge to the military leadership's presumed right to unquestioned authority, was the alternative version of patriotism embodied by the mothers, a version that defined the "good mother-citizen" as someone who stood up to the state. The UCSMR's activity deliberately promoted a subversive message that called for Russians to create a liberal state that would respect human rights, observe the rule of law, and adopt democratic principles.[39]

The UCSMR inspired the creation of other anti-military organizations, including the Social Organization in Defense of Human Rights, "Soldiers' Mothers of Saint Petersburg," the Interregional Movement "Soldiers' Mothers," and "Mothers' Right." In 2007, the Russian internet (*Runet*) hosted sixty-five anti-military websites categorized as: anti-military oriented to mothers; human-rights defense related to military service; aimed at youth by youth that are anti-war and anti-military; and businesses that for a fee help men avoid conscription both legally and illegally. They all had anti-authoritarian bents behind their willingness to assist potential conscripts with various legal, extra-legal, and illegal means of avoiding service and making the army follow the law.[40] The grassroots work of the mothers was in sync with a broad swath of society as revealed in a 2003 Levada Center poll that asked about military reform. The top four concerns that respondents prioritized were: the need to end violence between soldiers; improve living conditions for soldiers; transition as soon as possible to a volunteer army; and in the meantime, reduce the length of conscripted service.[41]

The September 2022 mobilization of reservists for the war in Ukraine, which affected at least 100,000 married men, led wives to create another organization, the All-Russian Council of Mothers and Wives (ARCMW). Its stated purpose was to hold the army accountable for violations of mobilization laws, and laws and regulations governing military service. The over 20,000 members who subscribed to its *Telegram* social media platform collected and disseminated information about the army sending unprepared reservists and conscripts to the front line, insufficient supplies of uniforms and equipment, problems with housing and food, and men being coerced into signing contracts. At the council's first meeting, it passed a resolution declaring their distrust of "the system of power that has dragged our country into a bloody armed conflict." The ARCMW called the country's leadership corrupt and accused it of suppressing human rights activity and public criticism, and of passing repressive laws that "strike the people in their fundamental rights, including freedom of speech and opinion."[42]

Feeling threatened by the challenge to its authority and the potential to undermine the war effort, the Putin regime moved to protect the Ministry of Defense against civilian criticism by outlawing the UCSMR in February 2022. The regime subsequently outlawed protests concerning the treatment of soldiers, labeling it "discrediting the army." These laws, which branded the UCSMR and other humanitarian nongovernmental organizations as "foreign agents" or "undesirable organizations," allowed the regime to legally end the organized activity of all human rights organizations in Russia by mid-2023. Until then, feeling the need to defuse the growing criticism of the mobilization and to appear reasonable and concerned about women's complaints, Putin held a well-publicized meeting in November 2022, five days before Russia's Mothers' Day, with a supposedly representative group of sixteen mothers of Russian soldiers. In fact, eleven turned out to be pro-Putin officials, deputies, functionaries of the All-Russian People's Front, and other government organizations.

The other five were vetted beforehand to be pro-Putin. It turns out that only three of the women had sons recently mobilized into the army. No members of the Council of Mobilized Mothers and Wives or the Union of Committees of Soldiers' Mothers of Russia were invited to the meeting.[43] Subsequently, the ARCMW was forced to disband in July 2023.

Refusing to be silenced, soldiers' wives and mothers created a new movement, *Put' domoi* (The Way Home), later outlawed in June 2024. Women in this group wore white scarves and placed flowers on monuments to soldiers as a silent but visible protest to the war. As the war dragged on into its third year, Mothers and wives continued to complain and ask accusingly: "Where is my son? Where is my husband? When, where, how, why did he die? Is this war necessary? Why are they being sent without proper equipment and weaponry? Their questions went unanswered, heightening popular distrust of the army and government.

CONCLUSION

Since the founding of the Imperial Russian Army by Peter I in the 1690s, Russian society's relationship with the military has been ambivalent, but mostly negative. The reasons are three-fold: the army, until recently, was used as a tool of repression by the state; military service has historically been unhealthy, brutal, unrewarding, and lowly regarded; and the officer corps has arrogantly held itself above reproach, even in the face of proven corruption and incompetence. In the 165 years since the emancipation of the serfs, the peoples of Russia have raised their expectations of military service. They expect soldiers to be treated humanely. They want the leadership to be held accountable for their treatment of the men and for dishonest behavior. They want military service to be only voluntary and decently paid. These expectations have not been met, thus reinforcing skeptical attitudes toward the army and its leaders, and eliciting sympathy for those who do not want to serve.

Overall, we can conclude that despite the best efforts of successive regimes—Alexander II and Dmitrii Miliutin in Imperial Russia, idealistic ideologues of the early Bolshevik years, and Gorbachev's and Yeltsin's liberal reformers—to improve the soldiers' lot, the Russian people will continue to have an ambivalent relationship with their army, in which the negative outweighs the positive because the life of the Russian soldier continues to be unenviable. The reason for this is that the culture of the military leadership remains one of self-satisfied superiority with disregard for human life and dignity. The officer corps has always considered hardship and deprivation to be an integral aspect of soldiering—for the rank and file—and therefore does not feel compelled to ameliorate conditions. While the degree and nature of hardship has evolved over the centuries, the underlying thought that a soldier's life *should* be hard and unrewarding, and that soldiers and society should accept this without complaint remains the fundamental outlook of the Russian military institution—and so, keeps Russian society from truly respecting the army.

No government has seen fit to use its power to force change. Instead, since the early years of the twentieth century, they have sought to change popular perceptions by investing in patriotic education. So far, all attempts to militarize society, particularly youth, have failed to persuade the people to accept the army on the army's terms. The consequences of government inaction are the failure to transition to an all-volunteer army, a process that, begun in the 1990s, after thirty years is still incomplete and the fact that a large percentage of the population condone service avoidance. Freedom of expression, allowed in the 1980s, and the internet have empowered civilians, especially wives and mothers, to make known to society at large their discontent with the treatment of the men. Though volunteers signed up in large numbers to become *kontraktniki* during the war with Ukraine, they only joined because of fantastically high enlistment bonuses and increases in salary. The vast majority of these men expect to quit the army as soon as they are able.

In summary, success in war often brings an abstract sense of pride in the army, but otherwise the popular image of the army is a poor one. It is highly unlikely that the Russian people will embrace military service as worthwhile until the military culture of the officer corps and the barracks change.

NOTES

Chapter 1

1 Vladimir S. Trubetskoi, *A Russian Prince in the Soviet State: Hunting Stories, Letters from Exile, and Military Memoirs* (Evanston, IL: Northwestern University Press, 2006), 177.
2 Mark von Hagen, *Soldiers in the Proletarian Dictatorship: The Red Army and the Soviet Socialist State, 1917–1930* (Ithaca, NY: Cornell University Press, 1990).
3 V. K. Belobrodov, "Dnevnik novobrantsa," *Voenno-istoricheskii arkhiv*, no. 11 (119) (November 2009): 122.
4 Albert J. Beveridge, *The Russian Advance* (New York: Harper, 1904), 134.
5 Aleksandr M. Kruchinin, *Rossiiskii polk s finskim imenem. Ocherki istorii Orovaiskogo polka (1811–1920)* (Ekaterinburg: UMTs UPI, 2000), 74; Elise Kimerling Wirtschafter, "The Lower Ranks in the Peacetime Regimental Economy of the Russian Army, 1796–1855," *Slavonic and East European Review*, vol. 64, no. 1 (January 1986): 45, 46; V. A. Maidan, ed., *Istoriia pitaniia zashchitnika gosudarstva Rossiiskogo*, Vol. 1 (St. Petersburg: LIO, 2000), 159–98.
6 Elise K. Wirtschafter, "The Lower Ranks in the Peacetime Regimental Economy," *Slavonic and East European Review*, vol. 64, no. 1 (January 1986), 46.
7 A. I. Panov, "Eshche o vol'nykh rabotakh," in *Armiia i politika: Ofitserskii korpus v politicheskoi istorii Rossii 1900–1916 gg. Dokumenty i materialy*, Vol. 1 (Moscow: Vitiaz', 2002), 61.
8 Anton Denikin, *The Career of a Tsarist Officer: Memoirs, 1872–1916*. trans. Margaret Patoski (Minneapolis: University of Minnesota Press, 1975), 82.
9 John S. Curtiss, *The Russian Army under Nicholas I, 1825–1855* (Durham, NC: Duke University Press, 1965), 250; Petr A. Zaionchkovskii, *Voennye reformy 1860–70 godov v Rossii* (Moscow, 1972), 38; John L. H. Keep, *Soldiers of the Tsar: Army and Society in Russia, 1462–1874* (Oxford: Clarendon, 1985), 374; V. S. Bobriyshev, et al., *Peterburgskii, Petrogradskii, Leningradskii voennyi okrug 1864–1999* (St. Petersburg: Poligon, 1999), 24; Maksim B. Olenev, *Russkaia armiia kak ona est', bez prikras* (Moscow: Staraia Basmannaia, 2021), 140.

Notes

10 Aleksei Bezugol'nyi, Nikolai Kovalevskii, and Valerii Kovalev, *Istoriia voenno-okruzhnoi sistemy v Rossii. 1862-1918* (Moscow: ZAO Izdatel'stvo Tsentropoligraf, 2012), 189-90, 245.
11 George E. Snow, "Alcoholism in the Russian Military: The Public Sphere and the Temperance Discourse, 1883-1917," *Jahrbücher für Geschichte Osteuropas*, vol. 45 (1997): 425.
12 Ibid., 418-20, 423-6.
13 Frank T. Csongos, "Red Army Alcoholism, Drug Abuse," *United Press International*, April 12, 1982, https://www.upi.com/Archives/1982/04/12/Red-Army-alcoholism-drug-abuse/2125387435600/. Accessed May 12, 2022.
14 Robert B. Davis, "Alcohol Abuse and the Soviet Military," *Armed Forces and Society*, vol. 11, no. 3 (Spring 1985): 403-5.
15 *Katekhizis russkogo soldata*, "Dukh soldata," in Kamenev, *Entsiklopediia russkogo ofitsera*, 1:622-5.
16 Peter Brock and John L. H. Keep, eds., *Life in a Penal Battalion of the Imperial Russian Army: The Tolstoyan N, T. Iziumchenko's Story* (York, UK: William Sessions, 2001), 12-13.
17 Henri Troyat, *Daily Life in Russia under the Last Tsar* (Stanford, CA: Stanford University Press, 1961), 119-20.
18 Brock and Keep, eds., *Life in a Penal Battalion of the Imperial Russian Army*, 28-32; Vladimir Iliuchik, "Izdevalsia slovesno i fizichecheski. Pokazyval, chto ia zdes' glavnyi," *Novaia gazety Evropa*, February 15, 2024, https://novayagazeta.eu/articles/2024/02/15/izdevalsia-slovesno-i-fizicheski-pokazyval-chto-ia-zdes-glavnyi. Accessed June 3, 2024.
19 Vladimir A. Petrov, *Ocherki po istorii revoliutsionnogo dvizheniia v russkoi armii v 1905 g.* (Moscow: 1964), 198-201, 202-3, 207-8, 210-11, 212-13, 217-21, 226-8, 229-31, 238.
20 Elisabeth Sieca-Kozlowski, "Introduction – The Relation of the Post-Soviet Army to Muslim Minorities," *The Journal of Power Institutions in Post-Soviet Societies*, no. 10 (2009): https://doi.org/10.4000/pipss.3767. Accessed May 10, 2024.
21 Liisi Esse, "Estonian Soldiers in World War I: A Distinctive Experience of a Small Nation in the Russian Army," in *Military Affairs in Russia's Great War and Revolution, 1914-1922*, ed., Laurie Stoff (Bloomington, IN: Slavica, 2019), 53, 54.
22 Alena Maklak, "Dedovshchina on trial. Some evidence concerning the last Soviet generation of 'sons' and 'grandfathers'," *Nationalities Papers*, vol. 43, no. 5 (2015): 689, http://dx.doi.org/10.1080/00905992.2015.1048676. Accessed May 11, 2024.
23 "Rossiia ukrepliaet armiiu i flot," *Krasnaia zvezda*, March 19, 2011.

Notes

24 Oksana Smirnova, "Russia's Prison Culture: Inside and Out," *The Moscow Times*, November 23, 2001, https://www.themoscowtimes.com/archive/russias-prison-culture-inside-and-out. Accessed July 16, 2024.

25 Svetlana Stephenson, "From the Streets to the Kremlin, Russia's Gang Culture Defines Strength," *The Moscow Times*, January 10, 2024, https://www.themoscowtimes.com/2024/01/10/from-the-streets-to-the-kremlin-russias-gang-culture-defines-strength-a83615. Accessed July 16, 2024.

26 Ibid.

27 Maklak, "Dedovshchina on trial," 690.

28 Julie Elkner, "Dedovshchina and the Committee of Soldiers' Mothers under Gorbachev," *The Journal of Power Institutions of Post-Soviet Societies*, no. 1 (2004); "SK vozbudil delo po faktu smerti 21-letnego srochnika v Volgogradskoi oblasti. On soobshchal o 'problemakh s sosluzhivtsami,'" *Novaia gazeta.eu*, June 29, 2022; Petr Aleshkovskii, "'Vse vsë znaiut,' Dnevnik pisatelia Petra Aleshkovskogo o tom, kak izmenilas' glubinnaia Rossiia za chetyre mesiatsa s nachala voiny," *Novaia gazeta Evropa*, June 25, 2022, https://novayagazeta.eu/articles/2022/06/25/vse-vsio-znaiut. Accessed June 25, 2022. Jennifer Gould, "Soldier's Mothers Fight Deadly Army Hazing," *The Moscow Times*, August 21, 1992, https://www.themoscowtimes.com/archive/soldiers-mothers-fight-deadly-army-hazing. Accessed October 17, 2024.

29 Anna Politkovskaya, *A Dirty War: A Russian Reporter in Chechnya* (London: Harvill, 2001), 46.

30 Larisa Deriglazova, "To Fear or to Respect? Two Approaches to Military Reform in Russia," *The Journal of Power Institutions in Post-Soviet Societies*, no. 3 (2005): https://doi.org/10.4000/pipss.415. Accessed April 3, 2023.

31 Katia Lakova, ed., "Zhaloby prezidentu na voinu," *Istories.media*, June 9, 2022, https://www.istories.media/investigations/2022/06/09/million-zhalob-prezidentu/. Accessed June 2, 2024.

Chapter 2

1 "Army 20 percent understaffed," *Moscow News.ru*, June 9, 2012. http://www.moscownews.ru/russia/20120609/189824693.html. Accessed November 20, 2022; Aleksandras Budrys, "Over 240,000 Russian men dodged draft last year," *Moscow News.ru*, March 13, 2013, http://www.moscownews.ru/russia/20130313/191333536/Over-240000-Russian-men-dodged-draft-last-year.html. Accessed November 20, 2022.

Notes

2 Elise Kimerling Wirtschafter, *From Serf to Russian Soldier* (Princeton, NJ: Princeton, University Press, 1990), 3.

3 Maksim B. Olenev, *Komplektovanie armii nizhnimi chinami pri imperatore Nikolae I* (Moscow: Staraia Basmannaia, 2006), 3–9; Fedor N. Ivanov, *Istoriia rekrutskoi povinnosti v Rossii (1699–1874 gg.)* (Moscow: Pervo, 2017), 46–7.

4 Wirtschafter, *From Serf to Russian Soldier*, 21–2.

5 Rodney D. Bohac, "The Mir and the Military Draft," *Slavic Review*, vol. 47, no. 4 (Winter 1988): 655.

6 Janet M. Hartley, *Russia, 1762–1825: Military Power, the State, and the People* (Westport, CT: Praeger, 2008), 31, 32.

7 Bohac, "The Mir and the Military Draft," 656; Wirtschafter, *From Serf to Russian Soldier*, 5–8, 24.

8 V. K. Belobrodov, "Dnevnik novobrantsa," *Voenno-istoricheskii arkhiv*, no. 11 (119) (November 2009): 112.

9 K. A. Stepanov, "Iaroslavskoe opolchenie v Otechestvennoi voine 1812 g.," *Voprosy Istorii*, no. 9 (2009): 146. Even in these times of national emergency, serf owners were not above putting their self-interest before the national interest by contributing fewer than the required number of men to the *opolchenie*.

10 Ivanov, *Istoriia rekrutskoi povinnosti v Rossii (1699–1874 gg.)*, 49–50, 51; Bohac, "The Mir and the Military Draft," 653, 657–65; Hartley, *Russia, 1762–1825*, 34, 35, 81; Wirtschafter, *From Serf to Russian Soldier*, 19.

11 *Lieven Papers*, vol. CCXI, addition ms 47427, The British Library, pages 9–10; Bohac, "The Mir and the Military Draft," 657–58; Beatrice Farnsworth, "The *Soldatka*: Folklore and Court Record," *Slavic Review*, vol. 49, no. 1 (Spring 1990), 70.

12 Hartley, *Russia, 1762–1825*, 79.

13 S. N. Rudnik, ed., "Raport starshego chinovnika osobykh poruchenii Vinogradova kostromoskomu gubernatoru V. I. Dorgobuzhinovu," *Istoricheskii arkhiv*, no. 1 (2014), 175–8; Ellen Jones, "Social Change and Civil-Military Relations," in *Soldiers and the Soviet State: Civil-Military Relations from Brezhnev to Gorbachev*, eds, Timothy J. Colton and Thane Gustafson (Princeton, NJ: Princeton University Press, 1990), 256; Iva Savic, "The Russian Soldier Today," *Journal of International Affairs*, vol. 63, no. 2 (Spring/Summer 2010): 220–1.

14 Wirtschafter, *From Serf to Russian Soldier*, 4–5, 7.

15 S. N. Rudnik, ed., "Ves'ma mnogo slukhov i tolkov o vziatochnichestve pri prizyve: Kak v Kostromskoi gubernii pytalis' izbezhat' prizyva na sluzhbu v armiiu. 1874 g.," *Istoricheskii arkhiv*, no. 1 (2014): 172–89; Aleksandr B. Astashov, "Chlenovreditel'stvo i simuliatsiia boleznei

Notes

v russkoi armii vo vremia Pervoi mirovoi voiny," *Novyi istoricheskii vestnik*, vol. 34, no. 4 (2012): 7; "Sud prigovoril khokkeista kluba 'Salavat Iulaev' Suleimanova k piati godam uslovno za pokupku voennogo bileta," *Novaia gazeta Evropa*, September 5, 2022, https://novayagazeta.eu/articles/2022/09/05/sud-prigovoril-khokkeista-kluba-salavat-iulaev-suleimanova-k-piati-godam-uslovno-za-pokupku-voennogo-bileta-news. Accessed September 6, 2022.

16 "Search for Term 'Kak slovat' ruku v domashnikh usloviiakh,'" September 2022.

17 Vladimir A. Kozlov, Sheila Fitzpatrick, and Sergei V. Mironenko, *Sedition: Everyday Resistance in the Soviet Union under Khrushchev and Brezhnev* (New Haven, CT: Yale University Press, 2011), 163.

18 Dale R. Herspring, *The Kremlin & the High Command: Presidential Impact on the Russian Military from Gorbachev to Putin* (Lawrence: University Press of Kansas, 2006), 44.

19 Larisa Deriglazova, "To Fear or to Respect? Two Approaches to Military Reform in Russia," *The Journal of Power Institutions in Post-Soviet Societies*, no. 3 (2005): https://doi.org/10.4000/pipss.415.

20 Alexander M. Golts and Tonya L. Putnam, "State Militarism and its Legacies: Why Military Reform Has Failed in Russia," *International Security*, vol. 29, no. 2 (Fall 2004): 154–5.

21 Ilya Volzhsky, "'No patriotism to be found there:' Russia planned to recruit 400,000 volunteer soldiers to the war by the end of the year. But the campaign doesn't seem to be going so well," *Novaya gazeta*, July 22, 2023, https://novayagazeta.eu/articles/2023/07/22/theres-no-patriotism-to-be-found-there-en. Accessed July 23, 2023.

22 Pavel P. Shcherbinin, "Soldatskie zheny v XVIII—nachale XX v.: opyt rekonstruktsii sotsial'nogo statusa, pravovogo polozheniia, sotsiokul'turnogo oblika, povedeniia i nastroenii," *The Journal of Power Institutions in Post-Soviet Societies*, nos. 4/5 (2006): https://doi.org/10.4000/pipss.448. Accessed July 22, 2023.

23 Ibid.

24 Farnsworth, "The *Soldatka*," 59–66.

25 Shcherbinin, "Soldatskie zheny v XVIII—nachale XX;" Wirtschafter, *From Serf to Russian Soldier*, 36, 38; Hartley, *Russia, 1762–1825*, 39–42.

26 Mark Baker, "Rampaging *Soldatki*, Cowering Police, Bazaar Riots and Moral Economy: The Social Impact of the Great War in Kharkiv Province," *Canadian-American Slavic Studies*, vol. 35, nos. 2–3 (Summer–Fall 2001): 143; Corinne Gaudin, "Rural Echoes of World War I: War Talk in the Russian Village," *Jahrbücher für Geschichte Osteuropas*, Neue Folge, vol. 56, no. 3 (2008): 410.

Notes

27 Sarah Badcock, "Women, Protest, and Revolution: Soldiers' Wives in Russia During 1917," *International Review of Social History*, vol. 49, no. 1 (April 2004): 62, 66, 67, 68.

28 Vladimir Dmitrenko and B. I. Zverev, *Armiia i obshchestvo. 1900–1941 gg. Stat'i, dokumenty* (Moscow: Institut rossiiskoi istorii RAN, 1999), 372–3.

29 *Rossia i natsional'no-osvoboditel'naia bor'ba na Balkanakh, 1875–1878* (Moscow: Nauka, 1978), 238–69, 313, 390–1; Andrei V. Kvitka, *Dnevnik zabaikal'skogo kazach'ego ofitsera*; *Russko-iaponskaia voina 1904–1905 gg.* (Moscow: Kuchkovo Pole, 2016), 120; T. G. Ageeva, "Uchastie 187th pekhotnogo Avarskogo polka v boevykh deistviiakh v period pervoi mirovoi voiny," in *Voennaia istoriia Rossii: problemy, poiski, resheniia: materialy Mezhdunarodnoi nauchno-prakticheskoi konferentsii, posviashchennoi 100-lntiiu Pervoi mirovoi voiny, g. Volgograd, 26–27 sentiabria 2014 g.*, ed., S. G. Sidorov (Volgograd: Volgogradskii gosudarstvennyi universitet, 2014), 271–82; Aleksandr M. Kruchinin, *Rossiiskii polk s finskim imenem. Ocherki istorii Orovaiskogo polka (1811–1920)* (Ekaterinburg: UMTs UPI, 2000), 80, 103, 119; Roger R. Reese, "What to Give: Popular Response in the Soviet Union to the Warm Clothes Drive during the Great Patriotic War," *Jahrbucher für Geschichte Osteuropas*, vol. 63, no. 3 (2015): 3–4.

30 "Kak 'mamochki' obespechivaiut rossiiskuiu armiiu vmesto Minoborony," *Vazhnye istorii*, July 4, 2022, https://istories.media/reportages/2022/07/04/kak-mamochki-obespechivayut-rossiiskuyu-armiyu-vmesto-minoboroni/. Accessed July 5, 2022.

31 Dar'ia Talanova, "I v mal'chishke, i v devochonke est' po 200 gramm vzryvchatki. Kak v detskikh sadakh i shkolakh Rossii uchat liubit' voinu i dazhe verbuiut detei na front: Issledovanie 'Novoi-Evropa,'" *Novaia gazeta Evropa*, June 23, 2023, https://novayagazeta.eu/articles/2023/06/23/i-v-malchishke-i-v-devchonke-est-po-200-gramm-vzryvchatki. Accessed June 23, 2023.

32 Gaudin, "Rural Echoes of World War I," 400.

33 "Russia's courts have handed down more than 2,500 sentences to combatants in two years of the war. In half of the cases, the punishment was eased," *Novaya gazeta Europa*, April 11, 2024, https://meduza.io/news/2024/04/11/novaya-gazeta-evropa-rossiyskie-sudy-za-dva-gody-voyny-vynesli-bolee-2-5-tysyachi-prigovorov-uchastnikam-boevyh-deystviy-v-polovine-sluchaev-im-smyagchali-nakazanie; "'Vernuvshiisia s voiny zhitel' Krasnoiarskogo kraia bol'she sutok izbival byvshuiu zhenu i ubi lee," *Vetstka*, July 11, 2024. Accessed July 12, 2024.

Notes

34 "Pervyi rossiiskii region vyvel na ulitsy druzhiny iz 'boitsov SVO,'" *The Moscow Times*, July 26, 2024, https://www.moscowtimes.ru/2024/07/26/vprimore-sozdali-dobrovolcheskii-patrul-izuchastnikov-voini-a137919. Accessed July 29, 2024.

35 Giles MacDonogh, *After the Reich: The Brutal History of the Allied Occupation* (New York: Basic Books, 2007), 318.

Chapter 3

1 John L. H. Keep, *Soldiers of the Tsar: Army and Society in Russia 1462–1874* (Oxford: Clarendon Press, 1985), 232, 234.

2 Carol B. Steven, "The Officer Corps of Peter I's Army," *Russian History*, vol. 35, nos. 1/2 (Summer 2008): 85, 87, 88; Janet M. Hartley, *Russia, 1762–1825: Military Power, the State, and the People* (Westport, CT: Praeger, 2008), 48.

3 Maria Frolova, "Formirovanie ofitserkogo sostava Moskovskogo opolcheniia 1855 g." *Voprosy istorii*, no. 7 (2009): 96, 97, 98–100.

4 *Ogonëk*, no. 9 (February 26, 1911): 6; no. 1 (January 1, 1912); no. 32 (August 5, 1912): 13; no. 38 (September 16, 1913); no. 50 (December 15, 1913): 5; Andrei A. Mikhailov, *Obaianie Mundira* (Pskov: Pskovskaia oblastnaia tipografia, 2004), 228.

5 Vladimir S. Trubetskoi, *A Russian Prince in the Soviet State: Hunting Stories, Letters from Exile, and Military Memoirs* (Evanston: Northwestern University Press, 2006), 154.

6 *Ogonëk*, no. 23 (June 2, 1912): 9.

7 A. I. Panov, "Mnogo li ofitserskikh synovei sredi Ofiterov?" in *Armiia i politika: Ofitserskii korpus v politicheskoi istorii Rossii 1900–1916 gg. Dokumenty i materialy*. vol. 1 (Moscow: Vitiaz', 2002), 88–9.

8 Mikhailov, *Obaianie Mundira*, 225–6.

9 Robert V. Barylski, *The Soldier in Russian Politics: Duty, Dictatorship, and Democracy under Gorbachev and Yeltsin* (New Brunswick: Transaction, 1998), 54–5.

10 Mark von Hagen, *Soldiers in the Proletarian Dictatorship: The Red Army and the Soviet Socialist State, 1917–1930* (Ithaca, NY: Cornell University Press, 1990), 210–20.

11 Elena Lysak, "Servir ou combattre: que les femmes cherchent-elles dans l'armée russe," *The Journal of Power Institutions in Post-Soviet Societies*, no. 17 (2016): https://doi.org/10.4000/pipss.4187. Accessed January 21, 2023.

Notes

12. Anatoly S. Cherniaev, *My Six Years with Gorbachev: Notes from a Diary* (University Park: Penn State University Press, 2000), 116–18.
13. Christopher Cerf and Marina Albee, ed., *Small Fires: Letters from the Soviet People to Ogonyok Magazine 1987–1990* (New York: Summit, 1990), 71.
14. "Findings of the Commission of the USSR Congress of People's Deputies to Investigate the Events which Occurred in the City of Tbilisi, 9 April 1989," *Cold War International History Project Bulletin*, nos. 12/13 (Fall/Winter 2001): 35–48; Manfred Sapper, "Everyday Militancy in Russia: The Legacy of Militarized Socialism," *The Journal of Power Institutions in Post-Soviet Societies*, no. 3 (2005): https://doi.org/10.4000/pipss.381. Accessed January 21, 2023.
15. Stephen M. Meyer, "How the Threat (and the Coup) Collapsed: The Politicization of the Soviet Military," *International Security*, vol. 16, no. 3 (Winter, 1991–2): 35.
16. Brian D. Taylor, "The Soviet Military and the Disintegration of the USSR," *Journal of Cold War Studies*, vol. 5, no. 1 (Winter 2003): 17–66; René De La Pedraja, *The Russian Military Resurgence: Post-Soviet Decline and Rebuilding, 1992–2018* (Jefferson, NC: McFarland, 2019), 56–68.
17. Sapper, "Everyday Militancy in Russia."
18. "Eshche odin udar po 'dedovshchine,'" *Krasnaia zvezda*, no. 256, October 30, 1997.
19. Larisa Deriglazova, "To Fear or to Respect? Two Approaches to Military Reform in Russia," *The Journal of Power Institutions in Post-Soviet Societies*, no. 3 (2005): https://doi.org/10.4000/pipss.415. Accessed February 8, 2023.
20. Iurii Belousov, "Pod prismotrom materei," *Krasnaia zvezda*, no. 220, November 30, 2010; Iurii Belousov, "Za synovei – spacibo!," *Krasnaia zvezda*, no. 223, December 5, 2014; Andrei Sukhov, "Serdtse materi i serdtse garnizona," *Krasnaia zvezda*, no. 106, September 23, 2016. Accessed February 8, 2023.
21. Barylski, *The Soldier in Russian Politics*, 54–5, 355; Sapper, "Everyday Militancy in Russia."
22. Ekaterina Barkalova, "'Everyone is afraid' The Kremlin says it wants Russian soldiers who fought in Ukraine to take up 'leading positions' in government—so where are they?" *Vazhnye istorii*, July 29, 2024, https://meduza.io/en/feature/2024/07/29/everyone-is-afraid. Accessed July 29, 2024.
23. "Bolee 300 uchastnikov voiny s Ukrainov stali deputatami," *The Moscow Times*, September 9, 2024, https://www.moscowtimes.ru/2024/09/09/bolee-300-uchastnikov-voini-sukrainoi-stali-deputatami-a141679. Accessed September 9, 2024.

Notes

24 James Beardsworth, "Who Are Russia's Pro-War Bloggers and Why are they Important?" https://www.themoscowtimes.com/2022/09/14/explainer-who-are-russias-pro-war-bloggers-and-why-are-they-important-a78793. Accessed September 14, 2022.

25 Tor Bukkvoll, "Their Hands in the Till," *Armed Forces & Society*, vol. 34, no. 2 (January 2008), 265, 266.

26 Frederick A. Wellesley, *With the Russians in Peace and War: Recollections of a Military Attaché* (London: Eveleigh Nash, 1905), 121.

27 W. H.-H. Waters, *"Secret and Confidential:" The Experiences of a Military Attaché* (London: John Murray, 1926), 107, 157; *Ogonëk* no. 25 (1911): 6; *Ogonëk* no. 26 (1911): 14.

28 *Krasnaia zvezda*, 12, 14, 18, 24 September, 3 October, 1929; 10, 18 November 1925.

29 "Zamkomanduiushchego IuVO otpravili v SIZO po delu o korruptsii. Ego obviniaiut v trate deneg Minoborony na obustroistvo dachi," *Novaya Gazeta Europa*, July 29, 2022, https://novayagazeta.eu/articles/2022/07/29/zamkomanduiushchego-iuvo-otpravili-v-sizo-po-delu-o-korruptsii-ego-obviniaiut-v-trate-deneg-minoborony-na-obustroistvo-dachi-news. Accessed July 29, 2022.

30 Dale R. Herspring, *The Kremlin & the High Command: Presidential Impact on the Russian Military from Gorbachev to Putin* (Lawrence: University Press of Kansas, 2006), 44, 82; Bukkvoll, "Their Hands in the Till," 265, 266.

31 Natalya Krinova, "Corruption in Armed Forces Climbs Fivefold," *The Moscow Times*, July 7, 2013, https://www.themoscowtimes.com/2013/07/11/corruption-in-armed-forces-climbs-fivefold-a25758. Accessed July 11, 2013; "Corruption in Russia's Military Quadrupled in 2018, Prosecutors Say," *The Moscow Times*, March 21, 2019, https://www.themoscowtimes.com/2019/03/21/corruption-in-russias-military-quadrupled-in-2018-prosecutors-say-a64907. Accessed March 22, 2019.

32 "'Budut arestovany sotni liudei.' Putin velel FSB zachistit' Minoborony, chtoby nakazat' za provably v Ukraine," *The Moscow Times*, May 24, 2024, https://www.moscowtimes.ru/2024/05/24/budut-arestovani-sotni-lyudei-putin-velel-fsb-zachistit-minoboroni-chtobi-nakazat-za-provali-v-ukraine-a131810. Accessed May 24, 2024.

33 Iurii Glushko and Alexander Kolesnikov, *Shkola rossiiskogo ofitserstva: istoricheskii spravochnik* (Moscow: Russki mir, 1993), 73–84, 119–50.

34 Albert J. Beveridge, *The Russian Advance* (New York: Harper, 1904), 135.

35 Vitali V. Penskoi, "Armiia Rossiiskoi imperii v XVIII v.: vybor model razvitiia," *Voprosy istorii*, no. 7 (2001): 123.

36 Eugene Miakinkov, *War and Enlightenment in Russia: Military Culture in the Age of Catherine II* (Toronto: University of Toronto Press, 2020), 134–5; Keep, *Soldiers of the Tsar*, 209.

Notes

37 Aleksei A. Ignat'ev, *A Subaltern in Old Russia*, trans. Ivor Montagu (London: Hutchinson, 1944), 87; I. N. Grebenkin, *Russkii ofitser v gody mirovoi voiny i revoliutsii: 1914–1918 gg.* (Riazan': Riazan' State University, 2010), 72; I. N. Grebenkin, "The disintegration of the Russian Army in 1917: Factors and Actors in the Process," *Russian Studies in History*, vol. 56, no. 3 (2017): 175.

38 V. A. Strel'nikov, "Nyne…mozhno by otmenit' vsiakie telesnye nakazaniia v voiske?" Zaiska kniazia N. A. Orlova. 1861 g." *Istoricheskii arkhiv*, no. 4 (2015): 182–9.

39 Keep, *Soldiers of the Tsar*, 369.

40 Andrei V. Gushchin, *Russkaia armiia v voine 1904–1905 gg.: istoriko-antropologicheskoe issledovanie vliianiia vzaimootnoshenii voennosluzhashchikh na khod boevykh deistvii* (St. Petersburg, Renome, 2014), 130; Oleg Airapetov, "Revolution and revolt in the Manchurian armies, as perceived by a future leader of the White movement," in *The Russian Revolution of 1905: Centenary Perspectives*, eds., Jonathan D. Smele and Anthony Heywood (London: Routledge, 2005), 96–7.

41 Arkady Babchenko, *One Soldier's War*, trans. Nick Grove (New York: Grove, 2006), 299.

42 Ibid., 216.

43 Valery Dzutsev, "Report Slams Hazing in the Military," *The Moscow Times*, October 21, 2004; Simon Saradzhyan, "Officer Convicted in Hazing Cleanup," *The Moscow Times*, March 11, 1998, https://www.themoscowtimes.com/archive/officer-convicted-in-hazing-cleanup. Accessed July 1, 2024.

44 Herspring, *The Kremlin & the High Command*, 181.

45 Ekaterina Reznikov and Julia Balakhonova, "Some fight to the last ditch while others get rich: A Guide to the Ukrainian War," *Proekt*, May 23, 2022, https://www.proekt.media/en/investigation-en/names-of-the-russian-military-officers/. Accessed May 23, 2022.

46 Oksana Iablokova, "Military School Tarnished by Hazing to Close," *The Moscow Times*, January 27, 2006, https://www.themoscowtimes.com/archive/military-school-tarnished-by-hazing-to-close. Accessed July 2, 2024; Oksana Iablokova, "Hazing Opens a Door for Change," *The Moscow Times*, February 7, 2006, https://www.themoscowtimes.com/archive/hazing-opens-a-door-for-change. Accessed July 2, 2024.

47 Iablokov, "Hazing Opens a Door for Change"; Nabi Abdullaev, "Ivanov Says Hazing not Army's Fault," *The Moscow Times*, February 16, 2006, https://www.themoscowtimes.com/archive/ivanov-says-hazing-not-armys-fault. Accessed July 2, 2024; Andrei Bondarenko, "41-ia Armiia v litsakh," *Krasnaia zvezda*, no. 55, March 30, 2012.

Notes

48 De La Pedraja, *The Russian Military Resurgence*, 189–190.
49 Herspring, *The Kremlin & the High Command*, 181, 182.
50 Babchenko, *One Soldier's War*, 298.
51 Ibid., 332.
52 Aleksandr Baklanov, "Riadovoi, ubivshii vosem' sosluzhivtsev v Zabaikal'e, rasskazal o poborakh i ugrozakh iznasilovaniia. Ego otets govorit o dedovshchine, Minoborony vse otritsaet," *Meduza*, November 7, 2019, https://meduza.io/feature/2019/11/07/ryadovoy-ubivshiy-vosem-sosluzhivtsev-v-zabaykalie-rasskazal-o-poborah-i-ugrozah-iznasilovaniya-ego-otets-govorit-o-dedovschine-minoborony-vse-otritsaet. Accessed June 19, 2024.
53 "'Postoianno prikhoditsia skidybat'sia na podarki grebanym generalam,' *Novaia Gazeta Evropa* rasskazala, kak rossiiskie voennye polypaout na fronte otpuska i 'raneniia,'" *Novaia Gazeta Evropa*, November 28, 2023, https://meduza.io/feature/2023/11/28/postoyanno-prihoditsya-skidyvatsya-na-podarki-grebanym-generalam. Accessed November 28, 2023.

Chapter 4

1 M. V. Naidu, "Military Power, Militarism, and Militarization: An Attempt at Clarification and Classification," *Peace Research*, vol. 17, no. 1 (January, 1985): 2–3.
2 John Keep, "The Origins of Russian Militarism," *Cahiers du Monde russe et soviétique*, vol. 26, no. 1 (January–March, 1985): 7; Bryan Mabee and Srdjan Vucetic, "Varieties of Militarism: Towards a Typology," *Security Dialogue*, vol. 49, nos. 1–2 (2018): 98–101.
3 John R. Gillis, *The Militarization of the Western World* (New Brunswick, NJ: Rutgers University Press, 1989), 1–5.
4 Johanna Dahlin, "'No One is Forgotten, Nothing is Forgotten': Duty, Patriotism, and the Russian Search Movement," *Europe-Asia Studies*, vol. 69, no. 7 (September 2017): 1076.
5 "Putin Declares Patriotism Russia's only National Idea," *The Moscow Times*, February 4, 2016, https://www.themoscowtimes.com/2016/02/04/putin-declares-patriotism-russias-only-national-idea-a51705. Accessed May 3, 2020.
6 Michele A. Berdy, "Russia's Long Romance with Patriotism," *The Moscow Times*, February 5, 2016; Dahlin, "No One Is Forgotten, Nothing is Forgotten," 1085–6.
7 James Beardsworth, "'My Father Said I'm a Traitor Who Should be Shot First': War in Ukraine Splits Russian Families," *The Moscow Times*,

Notes

March 15, 2022, https://www.themoscowtimes.com/2022/03/15/my-father-said-im-a-traitor-who-should-be-shot-first-war-in-ukraine-splits-russian-families-a76937 Accessed March 17, 2022; Nadezhda Svetlova, translated by Eilish Hart, "'When the Blitzkrieg Failed, He Started to Have Doubts': The Kremlin's Invasion of Ukraine Put Some Russians at Odds with Their Loved Ones. For Others, it Brought Them Together," *Meduza.io*, March 10, 2022, https://meduza.io/feature/2022/03/07/kogda-blitskriga-ne-poluchilos-zyat-nachal-somnevatsya-kogda-vveli-sanktsii-perestal-podderzhivat-voynu. Accessed March 11, 2022.

8 Donald P. Wright, "'Clouds Gathering on the Horizon:' The Russian Army and the Preparation of the Imperial Population for War, 1906–1914," *The Journal of Military History*, vol. 83, no. 4 (2019): 1135–37, 1147; A. I. Panov, "Militarizatsiia shkol'noi molodezhi," *Armiia i politika: Ofitserskii korpus v politicheskoi istorii Rossii 1900–1916 gg. Dokumenty i materialy.* vol. 1 (Moscow: Vitiaz', 2002), 504–6, originally published in *Ofitserskaia zhizn'*, no. 227, July 10, 1910.

9 Aaron J. Cohen, *War Monuments, Public Patriotism, and Bereavement in Russia, 1905–2015* (Lanham, MD: Lexington, 2020), 147–82.

10 "Fundament gosudarstva i obshchestva," *Krasnaia zvezda*, no. 73, April 26, 2008.

11 Anastasia Iakovleva, "Vospitanie Patriotov," *Krasnaia Zvezda*, no. 117 (July 3, 2010).

12 Allyson Edwards, "Raising Cannon Fodder: Vladimir Putin Talks Endlessly about 'Loving the Motherland,' but the Kremlin's Education Philosophy has Both Eyes on the Battlefield in Ukraine," *Meduza*, December 20, 2022, https://meduza.io/en/feature/2022/12/21/raising-cannon-fodder. Accessed December 21, 2022.

13 Dar'ia Talanova, "Krovotochashchie rantsy," *Novaya gazeta Evropa*, September 1, 2022, https://novayagazeta.eu/articles/2022/09/01/krovotochashchie-rantsy. Accessed September 1, 2022.

14 Wright, "Clouds Gathering on the Horizon," 1139, 1141–2, 1145; "Voennaia gymnastika po cheshskoi 'sokol'skoi' sistem, vvedenaia v l.-Gv. S.-Peterburgskom polku," *Ogonëk*, no. 35 (1909):, 13; "Batal'on 'potyshnykh' voisk v novom Petergof, pod rukovodstvom ofitserov Kaspiiskago polka," *Ogonëk*, no. 29 (1910): 13; "Deti-soldaty i sestry miloserdiia" *Ogonëk*, no. 48 (1910): 13; "Vesenniaia zhizn' shkol'nikov," *Ogonëk*, no. 23 (1912): 16; *Ogonëk*, no. 35 (1909): 15; *Ogonëk*, no. 16 (1910): 23; *Ogonëk*, no. 32 (1910): 14–15.

15 Bella N. Sambur, "Voenno-Patrioticheskaia podgotovkai trudovoe ispol'zovanie podrostkovoi molodezhi nakanune i v nachale velikoi otechestvennoi voiny (na primere Stavropol'skogo kraia)," *Vestnik*

Notes

Kemerovskogo gosudarstvennogo universiteta, vol. 6, no. 2 (2015): 198; V. G. Kevtsov, "Sotsial'nye i organizatsionnye problem voennykh reform 20–30-x godov," in *Armiia i obshchestvo. 1900–1941 gg. Stat'i, dokumenty*, ed., Vladimir Dmitrenko, B. I. Zverev (Moscow: Institut rossiiskoi istorii RAN, 1999), 177.

16 Olga V. Galkova and Irina A. Petrova, "Militarizatsiia zhizni sovetskoi molodezhi v 1920-x—nachale 1930-x godov," *Vestnik Volgograd Gos. Univ.* vol. 4, no. 4 (2015): 12–13.

17 Ibid., 18.

18 Andrei Kurnaiaiev, "Vremia patriotov," *Krasnaia zvezda*, no. 18, February 3, 2007; Marina Eliseeva, "Iunarmeiskii pochin," *Krasnaia zvezda*, no. 54, May 23, 2016.

19 Jonna Alava, "Russia's Young Army: Raising New Generations into Militarized Patriots," in *Nexus of Patriotism and Militarism in Russia: A Quest for Internal Cohesion*, ed., Katri Pynnöniemi (Helsinki: Helsinki University Press, 2021), 253, 263, 267–8, 270; Daria Talanova, "Kolybel' voiny," *Novaya gazeta Evropa*, October 15, 2024, https://novayagazeta.eu/articles/2024/10/15/kolybel-voiny. Accessed October 31, 2024.

20 Marina Vinogradskaya, "Avtomat v rukakh derzhat' i ot puli pogibat' uchat v shkole, uchat v shkole, uchat v shkole. Noveishaia istoriia militarizatsii rossiiskikh podrostkov," *Novaya Gazeta. Europe*, November 14, 2022, https://novayagazeta.eu/articles/2022/11/14/avtomat-v-rukakh-derzhat-i-ot-puli-pogibat-uchat-v-shkole-uchat-v-shkole-uchat-v-shkole. Accessed November 14, 2022.

21 Vladislav Ia. Grosul, "Russian Society and the Crimean War," *Russian Studies in History*, vol. 51, no. 1 (Summer 2012): 43, 57–8.

22 Michael Melancon, *The Socialist Revolutionaries and the Russian Antiwar Movement 1914–1917* (Columbus: The Ohio State University Press, 1990), 113–89; S. N. Bazanov, *Antivoennye vystupleniia na russkom fronte v 1917 godu glazami sovremennikov (vospominaniia, dokumenty, komentarii)* (Moscow: RAN, 2010).

23 Kristina Safonova, "'Normal'nyi chelovek ne mozhet bystupat' protiv voiny:' Vo vremiia vtorzheniia v Afganistan zhitelei SSSR presledovali za antivoennye stikhi, listovki i prosto razgovory. *Meduza* rasskazyvaet, kak eto bylo–i pochemu spustia 40 let povtorilos' vnov'," *Meduza*, April 26, 2023, https://meduza.io/feature/2023/04/26/normalnyy-chelovek-ne-mozhet-vystupat-protiv-voyny. Accessed April 26, 2023; Yaacov Ro'i, *The Bleeding Wound: The Soviet-Afghan War and the Collapse of the Soviet System* (Stanford, CA: Stanford University Press, 2022), 170.

24 Melissa Urban, "1995: Russian Mothers Attempt to Stop Chechen War," https://libcom.org/article/1995-russian-mothers-attempt-stop-chechen-war. Accessed April 3, 2022.

Notes

25 Anna Fillipova, "'Putinskaia Rossiia–zhivoi zakoldovannyi trup:' Odnoi iz samykh zametnykh antivoennykh organizatsii v rossii stalo 'Feministskoe soprotivlenie.' Vot ego istoriia," *Meduza,* March 22, 2022.

26 Yuri Terekhov, "Kennan Cable no. 84: A Survey of Russian Grassroots Anti-War Resistance," (Washington DC:Wilson Center, 2023). https://www.wilsoncenter.org/sites/default/files/media/uploads/documents/Cable84_v3.pdf. Accessed November 12, 2022.

27 "Feminist Anti-war Resistance Movement Demands Russian Troops' Withdrawal from Ukraine," *Meduza,* November 27, 2022, https://meduza.io/en/news/2022/11/27/feminist-anti-war-resistance-movement-demands-russian-troops-withdrawal-from-ukraine. Accessed November 11, 2022.

28 "20 tysych zaderzhanii." *Meduza* February 22, 2024, https://meduza.io/feature/2024/02/22/20-tysyach-zaderzhaniy-900-ugolovnyh-del-267-chelovek-za-reshetkoy-chetyre-s-polovinoy-goda-sredniy-srok-lisheniya-svobody. Accessed Febrary 23, 2024; "V rossiiskie sudy postupilo bol'she 8 tysyach administrativnykh del o 'discreditatsii' armii," *Mediazona,* October 10, 2023, https://zona.media/news/2023/10/10/8k-2033. Accessed October 10, 2023.

29 Roger R. Reese, "Eastern Europe's Reluctant Soldiers: Recruitment to the Armies of the Warsaw Pact, 1956–1991," in *Propaganda and Public Relations in Military Recruitment: Promoting Military Service in the Twentieth and Twenty-First Centuries,* ed. Brendan Maarten and Thomas Blivin (London: Routledge, 2021), 131–44; Dale R. Herspring, *The Kremlin & the High Command: Presidential Impact on the Russian Military from Gorbachev to Putin* (Lawrence: University Press of Kansas, 2006), 148.

30 Matthew Bodnar, "Russians Learn to Love the Army," *The Moscow Times,* February 20, 2017, https://www.themoscowtimes.com/2017/02/20/russians-learn-to-love-the-army-a57210. Accessed March 1, 2023.

31 Reese, "Eastern Europe's Reluctant Soldiers," 131–44; M. Steven Fish, "Reform and Demilitarization in Soviet Society from Brezhnev to Gorbachev," *Peace & Change,* vol. 15, no. 2 (April 1990): 163, 164, 166.

32 "In Photos: Russian High Schoolers Undergo Basic Military, First Aid Training," *The Moscow Times,* April 7, 2023, https://www.themoscowtimes.com/2023/04/07/in-photos-russian-high-schoolers-undergo-basic-military-and-first-aid-training-a80751. Accessed April 9, 2023.

33 Marina Vinogradskaia, "Blind Patriotism 101: Why the 'Special Military Operation' Disappeared from the New Cycle of Lessons Intended to 'Instill Patriotism' in Russian Schools," *Novaya Gazeta. Europe,* September 17, 2022, https://novayagazeta.eu/articles/2022/09/17/blind-patriotism-101. Accessed September 17, 2022.

34 "Starshim shkol'nikam naplevat', a mladshim vse ravno.' Kak putinskie uroki nenavisti, 'Iunarmiia' i prochaia dich' drizhivaiutsia v srednei shkole," *Vazhnye istorii*, November 22, 2022, https://istories.media/stories/2022/11/22/starshim-shkolnikam-naplevat-a-mladshim-vse-ravno/. Accessed November 23, 2022; Iuliia Akhmedova, "'Tysiachi shkol'nikov ostalis' bez prepodavatelei': kak voina b'et po obrazovaniiu," *Verstka*, October 9, 2022, https://verstka.media/mobilizaciya-uchitley-voyna-i-obrazovanie. Accessed October 10, 2022; "'Your Child has to Spend a Lot of Time with these Adults.' How Russia's Young War Opponents Navigate a School System Set on Churning out Putin Supporters," *Meduza*, November 21, 2022, https://meduza.io/en/feature/2022/11/21/your-child-has-to-spend-a-lot-of-time-with-these-adults. Accessed November 21, 2022.
35 Ekaterina Krasotkina, "S sistemoi nel'zia borot'sia: ona sil'nee," *Meduza*, November 13, 2024, https://meduza.io/feature/2024/11/13/s-sistemoy-nelzya-borotsya-ona-silnee-a-vot-esli-podtachivat-ee-iznutri-eto-rabotaet. Accessed November 13, 2024.
36 "The War in Chechnya and Russian Civil Society: Briefing of the Commission on Security and Cooperation in Europe," (Washington DC, 2005), https://web.archive.org/web/20081126150307/http://csce.gov/index.cfm?FuseAction=ContentRecords.ViewWitness&ContentRecord_id=495&ContentType=D&ContentRecordType=D&ParentType=B&CFID=5163160&CFTOKEN=65570212. Accessed November 12, 2023; Evan Gershkovich, "Russia's Fast-Growing 'Youth Army' Aims to Breed Loyalty to the Fatherland," *The Moscow Times* April 17, 2019, https://www.themoscowtimes.com/2019/04/17/russias-fast-growing-youth-army-aimst-to-breed-loyalty-to-the-fatherland-a65256. Accessed April 19, 2019.
37 "'U vsekh kontuzia legkoi ili srednei stepeni tiazhesti:' zheny buriatskikh voennykh poprosili glavu regiona vernut' ikh suprugov iz Ukrainy domoi," *Novaia gazeta Evropa*, June 28, 2022; https://www.youtube.com/watch?v=hfzVceKrbTU&t=48s. Accessed June 30, 2022. The protest was successful; in July the army flew 100 Buriat soldiers home.
38 "The War in Chechnya and Russian Civil Society" (Washington, DC, 2005).
39 Amy Caiazza, *Mothers and Soldiers: Gender, Citizenship, and Civil Society in Contemporary Russia* (Boca Raton, FL: Taylor & Francis, 2002), 124, 126.
40 Markku Lonkila, "The Internet and Anti-Military Activism in Russia," *Europe-Asia Studies*, vol. 60, no. 7 (September, 2008): 1125, 1129, 1132–3, 1145, 1146.

Notes

41 Larisa Deriglazova, "To Fear or to Respect? Two Approaches to Military Reform in Russia," *The Journal of Power Institutions in Post-Soviet Societies*, no. 3 (2005), https://doi.org/10.4000/pipss.415. Accessed February 8, 2024.

42 "Russian Social Network Bans Soldiers' Mothers' Group Following Putin Criticism," *The Moscow Times*, November 28, 2022, https://www.themoscowtimes.com/2022/11/28/russian-social-network-bans-soldiers-mothers-group-following-putin-criticism-a79516. Accessed November 30, 2022; Sofia Orlova, " 'The Country is in Trouble, and this is not some Private Issue.' How the 'Council of Mothers and Wives' Appeared, Criticizing the Mobilization, the Failed Tactics of the Special Operation, 5G Towers, and also Advocating the Revival of the USSR," *Novaia gazeta Evropa*, December 20, 2022, https://novayagazeta.eu/articles/2022/12/20/v-strane-to-beda-i-eto-ne-kakoi-to-chastnyi-vopros. Accessed December 22, 2022.

43 Andrei Pertsev, "A 'Necessary Quantity of Mothers' Putin Held a Highly Publicized Meeting with 'Mothers of the Mobilized.' Here's Who those Women Actually Are," *Meduza*, December 7, 2022.

SELECT BIBLIOGRAPHY

Babchenko, Arkady. *One Soldier's War*. Translated by Nick Grove. New York: Grove, 2006.

Badcock, Sarah. "Women, Protest, and Revolution: Soldiers' Wives in Russia During 1917." *International Review of Social History*, vol. 49, no. 1 (April 2004): 47–70.

Baker, Mark. "Rampaging *Soldatki*, Cowering Police, Bazaar Riots and Moral Economy: The Social Impact of the Great War in Kharkiv Province." *Canadian-American Slavic Studies*, vol. 35, nos. 2–3 (Summer–Fall 2001): 137–55.

Barylski, Robert V. *The Soldier in Russian Politics: Duty, Dictatorship, and Democracy under Gorbachev and Yeltsin*. New Brunswick: Transaction, 1998.

Beloborodov, V. K. "Dnevnik novobrantsa." *Voenno-istoricheskii arkhiv*, no. 11 (119) (November 2009): 110–29.

Bezugol'nyi, Aleksei, Nikolai Kovalevskii, and Valerii Kovalev. *Istoriia voenno-okruzhnoi sistemy v Rossii. 1862–1918*. Moscow: ZAO Izdatel'stvo Tsentropoligraf, 2012.

Bohac, Rodney D. "The Mir and the Military Draft." *Slavic Review*, vol. 47, no. 4 (Winter 1988): 652–66.

Brock, Peter, and John L. H.Keep, eds., *Life in a Penal Battalion of the Imperial Russian Army: The Tolstoyan N, T. Iziumchenko's Story*. York, UK: William Sessions, 2001.

Caiazza, Amy. *Mothers and Soldiers: Gender, Citizenship, and Civil Society in Contemporary Russia*. Boca Raton, FL: Taylor & Francis, 2002.

Cohen, Aaron J. *War Monuments, Public Patriotism, and Bereavement in Russia, 1905–2015*. Lanham, MD: Lexington, 2020.

Colton, Timothy J., and Thane Gustafson, eds., *Soldiers and the Soviet State: Civil-Military Relations from Brezhnev to Gorbachev*. Princeton, NJ: Princeton University Press, 1990.

Curtiss, John S. *The Russian Army under Nicholas I, 1825–1855*. Durham, NC: Duke University Press, 1965.

Dahlin, Johanna. " 'No one is Forgotten, Nothing is Forgotten': Duty, Patriotism, and the Russian Search Movement." *Europe-Asia Studies*, vol. 69, no. 7 (September 2017): 1070–89.

De La Pedraja, René. *The Russian Military Resurgence: Post-Soviet Decline and Rebuilding, 1992–2018*. Jefferson, NC: McFarland, 2019.

Select Bibliography

Denikin, Anton Ivanovich. *The Career of a Tsarist Officer: Memoirs, 1872–1916*. Translated by Margaret Patoski. Minneapolis: University of Minnesota Press, 1975.

Deriglazova, Larisa. "To Fear or to Respect? Two Approaches to Military Reform in Russia." *The Journal of Power Institutions in Post-Soviet Societies*, no. 3 (2005).

Dmitrenko, Vladimir and B. I. Zverev. *Armiia i obshchestvo. 1900–1941 gg. Stat'i, dokumenty*. Moscow: Institut rossiiskoi istorii RAN, 1999.

Elkner, Julie. "Dedovshchina and the Committee of Soldiers' Mothers under Gorbachev." *The Journal of Power Institutions of Post-Soviet Societies*, no. 1 (2004).

Farnsworth, Beatrice. "The *Soldatka*: Folklore and Court Record." *Slavic Review*, vol. 49, no. 1 (Spring 1980): 58–73.

Galkova, Olga V. and Irina A. Petrova. "Militarizatsiia zhizni sovetskoi molodezhi v 1920-x—nachale 1930-x godov." *Vestnik Volgograd Gos. Univ.*, vol. 4, no. 4 (2015): 8–18.

Grebenkin, I. N. "The disintegration of the Russian Army in 1917: Factors and Actors in the Process." *Russian Studies in History*, vol. 56, no. 3 (2017): 172–87.

Grebenkin, I. N. *Russkii ofitser v gody mirovoi voiny i revoliutsii: 1914–1918 gg*. Riazan': Riazan' State University, 2010.

Grosul, Vladslav Ia. "Russian Society and the Crimean War." *Russian Studies in History*, vol. 51, no. 1 (Summer 2012): 35–64.

Gillis, John R. *The Militarization of the Western World*. New Brunswick, NJ: Rutgers University Press, 1989.

Gushchin, Andrei V. *Russkaia armiia v voine 1904–1905 gg.: istoriko-antropologicheskoe issledovanie vliianiia vzaimoostnoshenii voennosluzhashchikh na khod boevykh deistvii*. St. Petersburg, Renome, 2014.

Hagen, Mark von. *Soldiers in the Proletarian Dictatorship: The Red Army and the Soviet Socialist State, 1917–1930*. Ithaca, NY: Cornell University Press, 1990.

Hartley, Janet M. *Russia, 1762–1825: Military Power, the State, and the People*. Westport, CT: Praeger, 2008.

Herspring, Dale R. *The Kremlin & the High Command: Presidential Impact on the Russian Military from Gorbachev to Putin*. Lawrence, KS: University Press of Kansas, 2006.

Ivanov, Fedor N. *Istoriia rekrutskoi povinnosti v Rossii (1699–1874 gg.)*. Moscow: Pervo, 2017.

Keep, John L. H. *Soldiers of the Tsar: Army and Society in Russia 1462–1874*. Oxford: Clarendon Press, 1985.

Select Bibliography

Keep, John L. H. "The Origins of Russian Militarism." *Cahiers du Monde russe et soviétique*, vol. 26, no. 1 (January–March 1985): 5–19.

Lonkila, Markku. "The Internet and Anti-Military Activism in Russia." *Europe-Asia Studies*, vol. 60, no. 7 (September 2008): 1125–49.

Mabee, Bryan, and Srdjan Vucetic. "Varieties of Militarism: Towards a Typology." *Security Dialogue*, vol. 49, nos. 1-2 (2018): 96–108.

Miakinkov, Eugene. *War and Enlightenment in Russia: Military Culture in the Age of Catherine II*. Toronto: University of Toronto Press, 2020.

Naidu, M. V. "Military Power, Militarism, and Militarization: An Attempt at Clarification and Classification." *Peace Research*, vol. 17, no. 1 (January 1985): 2–10.

"Nyne…mozhno by otmenit' vsiakie telesnye nakazaniia v voiske?" Zaiska kniazia N. A. Orlova. 1861 g." *Istoricheskii arkhiv*, no. 4 (2015): 182–9.

Olenev, Maksim B. *Russkaia armiia kak ona est', bez prikas*. Moscow: Staraia Basmannaia, 2021.

Olenev, Maksim B. *Komplektovanie armii nizhnimi chinami pri imperatore Nikolae I*. Moscow: Staraia Basmannaia, 2006.

Panov, A. I. *Armiia i politika: Ofitserskii korpus v politicheskoi istorii Rossii 1900–1916 gg. Dokumenty i materialy*. Vol. 1, Moscow: Vitiaz', 2002.

Politkovskaya, Anna. *A Dirty War: A Russian Reporter in Chechnya*. London: Harvill, 2001.

Pynnöniemi, Katri, ed., *Nexus of Patriotism and Militarism in Russia: A Quest for Internal Cohesion*. Helsinki: Helsinki University Press, 2021.

Ro'i, Yaacov. *The Bleeding Wound: The Soviet-Afghan War and the Collapse of the Soviet System*. Stanford, CA: Stanford University Press, 2022.

Rudnik, S. N., ed., "Ves'ma mnogo slukhov i tolkov o vziatochnichestve pri prizyve: Kak v Kostromskoi gubernii pytalis' izbezhat' prizyva na sluzhbu v armiiu. 1874 g." *Istoricheskii arkhiv*, no. 1 (2014): 172–89.

Shcherbinin, Pavel P. "Soldatskie zheny v XVIII—nachale XX v.: opyt rekonstruktsii sotsial'nogo statusa, pravovogo polozheniia, sotsiokul'turnogo oblika, povedeniia i nastroenii." *The Journal of Power Institutions in Post-Soviet Societies*, nos. 4/5 (2006).

Smele, Jonathan D., and Anthony Heywood, eds., *The Russian Revolution of 1905: Centenary Perspectives*. London: Routledge, 2005.

Steven, Carol B. "The Officer Corps of Peter I's Army." *Russian History*, vol. 35, nos. 1-2 (Summer 2008): 85–97.

Troyat, Henri. *Daily Life in Russia under the Last Tsar*. Stanford, CA: Stanford University Press, 1961.

Wirtschafter, Elise Kimerling. *From Serf to Russian Soldier*. Princeton, NJ: Princeton University Press, 1990.

Select Bibliography

Wirtschafter, Elise Kimerling. "The Lower Ranks in the Peacetime Regimental Economy of the Russian Army, 1796–1855." *Slavonic and East European Review*, vol. 64, no. 1 (January 1986): 40–65.

Wright, Donald P. "'Clouds Gathering on the Horizon:' The Russian Army and the Preparation of the Imperial Population for War, 1906–1914." *The Journal of Military History*, vol. 83, no. 4 (2019): 1133–60.

Zaionchkovskii, Petr A. *Voennye reformy 1860–70 godov v Rossii*. Moscow, 1972.

Online Sources

Meduza
The Moscow Times
Novaia Gazeta Evropa
Vazhnye istorii
Verstka

Archival Sources

Lieven Papers, vol. CCXI, addition ms 47427, The British Library.

INDEX

Abramkin, Valery 27, 28
alcohol 5, 14, 15, 36, 93
Alexander I 37
Alexander II 20, 60, 74, 87
Alexander III 23, 62
anti-militarism
   Chechen Wars inspired 96
   imperial period 87
   invasion of Ukraine inspired 98, 103
   politically inspired 63, 95
   Soviet-Afghan War inspired 65
   unleashed by *glasnost* 41, 54, 58, 65, 71
anti-Semitism 25, 49
anti-war activities
   Chechen wars related 96, 97
   invasion of Ukraine related 51, 97, 98, 100, 102
atrocities 53, 54, 65, 97
August Coup 54, 66

Babchenko, Arkady 75, 78
Bolshevik Party 8, 47, 63, 64, 88, 91
Bolshevik Revolution, *see* October Revolution
bribery
   among officers 70, 72, 79
   to avoid conscription 35, 39, 40, 43, 98

catechism of the soldier 16
Catherine II 33, 34, 40, 45, 59

Chechen wars 29, 41, 50, 75, 96, 97
Civil War, Russian 8, 37, 38, 47, 50
Cold War 7, 8, 13, 40, 67
Commissariat of Defense 75, 91
commissars 16, 17, 18, 63, 64
Committee of Soldiers' Mothers (CSM and UCSMR)
   founding 28
   Russian Federation period 30, 31, 67, 77, 103, 105
   Soviet era 29, 65, 66, 96, 97, 102
Communist Party 3, 8, 18, 52, 63
conscription
   imperial era 24, 34, 6, 36, 46
   Russian Federation period 42, 43, 84, 103
   Soviet era 7, 26, 41, 42, 49, 102
conscripts 6, 15
corporal punishment 14, 18, 20
corruption
   imperial era 70
   Russian Federation period 72, 79
   Soviet era 13, 65, 71, 72
crime
   by officers 63, 71, 72, 76, 78
   by soldiers 15, 18, 20, 53, 54
Crimean War 34, 51, 60, 96

Dahlin, Johanna 82
dedovshchina, see hazing
desertion 5, 10, 42, 53
DOSAAF 91, 92, 99
draft deferments 23, 41, 42, 43

Index

draft evasion
  imperial period 33, 41
  Russian Federation period 42, 93
  Soviet period 42
  toleration of 82, 98

February Revolution 12, 19, 47, 61
First World War 47, 51, 52, 96
food, *see* nutrition

glasnost 28, 41, 65
GlavPUR 18, 21, 64
Gorbachev, Mikhail
  policy of *glasnost* 28, 42
  reforms of 41, 65, 67, 96
  relation to armed forces 54, 66
Grebenik, Valentina 101

hazing
  Committee of Soldiers' Mothers criticism of 28, 30, 65, 102
  Russian Federation period 20, 77, 78
  Soviet era 6, 25, 26, 27
health of soldiers 13, 14
housing 5, 9, 12, 50

indoctrination
  military 6, 16
  political 8, 88
  youth 86, 93, 94, 99, 100
Important Conversations 90, 99, 100
Iunarmiia 92, 93, 101
Ivanov, Sergei 77

Kirbasova, Maria 96
Komsomol 88, 91, 93
kontraktniki 8, 26, 28, 43, 44

Law on Universal Military Obligation of 1874 23, 24, 34, 46, 60

Law on Universal Military Service of 1967 34
Lymar, Liubov 28

Melnikova, Valentina 103
milbloggers 69
militarism 82, 87, 95, 96, 99
militarization
  definition of 82
  imperial period 86
  school-based 89, 99, 100, 101
  societal response to 95
Miliutin, Dmitrii 34, 58, 60, 70, 74
Ministry of Defense
  imperial era 10, 57
  response to hazing 26, 29, 30, 77, 102
  role in youth indoctrination 92, 93, 94
  Russian Federation 14, 33, 43, 52, 68, 104
  Soviet era 41, 42, 66, 94
murder 5, 15, 26, 29, 54, 78
mutiny 19, 20, 21

nachal'noi voennoi podgotovki (pre-conscription training, NVP) 94, 95, 99, 100, 101
Naidu, M. V. 82
Nicholas I, Tsar 23, 33, 37, 60, 83
Nicholas II, Tsar 62, 86, 87
non-commissioned officers (NCOs) 5, 18, 20, 21
nutrition
  acquisition of 50
  insufficient amount 9, 12, 14, 21, 33, 104
  quality of 5, 9, 13

October Revolution 7, 12, 16, 83
officer corps
  imperial era 60, 61, 62

Index

Russian Federation 66, 67, 68, 69, 79
   self-image of 57, 58, 59
   Soviet era 63, 64, 65, 66
Oleinik, Anton 27
Osetrov, Vladimir 77
Osoaviakhim 90, 91

paika 46, 47, 48, 102
patriotic education 81, 87, 88, 89, 94
patriotism
   definition of 82, 83
   military service related to 43, 81, 86, 89, 91
   popular response to 85, 86, 103
   recruitment based on 44, 84
   youth the object of 87, 90, 92, 94, 101
pay
   officers' 59, 64, 67, 68, 70
   soldiers' 5, 8, 10, 11, 21, 44
Peter I, Tsar 2, 3, 9, 59
Peter III, Tsar 59
poteshnyi units 90
pre-conscription training, *see* NVP
Putin, Vladimir
   expectations of soldiers 55
   meeting with mothers 104
   patriotic program of 18, 84, 88, 89, 103
   relations with officers 57, 68, 69, 72
   suppression of NGOs 97
   use of prison slang 27

quartering, *see* housing

religion 17, 18, 22, 23, 24, 34
Revolution of 1905 12, 20, 21, 34, 51
Russian Orthodox Church 17, 18, 52
Russo-Japanese War 51, 52, 86, 96
Russo-Turkish War (1877–78) 51, 96

Second World War 7, 15, 19, 21, 48, 52
self-mutilation 39, 40, 41
Serdiukov, Anatoly 26
service avoidance 38, 42
Shamsutdinov, Ramil 78
Shoigu, Sergei 72
sokol clubs 90
soldatki 45, 46, 47
Soviet-Afghan War 40, 54, 65, 96
substitutes 38, 39
suicide 5, 14, 28, 29
Sychov, Andrei 77

Ukraine, Russian invasion of 40, 41, 44, 51, 52, 86
Union of Committees of Soldiers' Mothers of Russia (UCSMR), *see* Committee of Soldiers' Mothers (CSM)

volunteers 7, 9, 26, 34, 43, 44

Wirtschafter, Elise K. 33

Yeltsin, Boris 7, 66, 67, 76, 97